BODY MATTERS

Simple Secrets for
ELEGANT AGING

BODY MATTERS

Simple Secrets for
ELEGANT AGING

by

Darca Lee Nicholson, MA

"***BODY MATTERS*** is a valuable perspective from an
experienced healer. Darca Nicholson's wisdom
will light the way for many readers."

Larry Dossey, MD, Author:
*The Extraordinary Healing Power
of Ordinary Things*

Medical Disclaimer. All information in this book is of a general nature and is intended to support the reader's knowledge and understanding. This information is not to be taken as medical advice pertaining to readers' specific health or medical condition.

Overhead Press
P.O. Box 595
Ukiah, CA 95482

First edition 2007
Printed in U.S.A.

ISBN 9781873671306
Library of Congress Control Number: 2007921546

Book design: Joan Giannecchini. www.casanonnastudios.com and Darca Nicholson.

Cover design and mandala: David Todd, Bonnie Bell, www.gaiastarworld.com.

Photo: Patty Joslyn-Babic

Unless otherwise specified, all illustrations are by the author.

Dedication:
To my family of origin
To my friends for life
And for all eternity,
To my daughter,
Denali

THANK YOU.

Drawing of four diaphragms in our body:
soft palate, jaw, thoracic, urogenital

Body Matters
Simple Secrets for Elegant Aging

Table of Contents

GREAT ELLE HERON
Bunyoroyal Lake 2006

ACKNOWLEDGMENTS

Thank you to my dear friends who gave me sanctuary during the years of bringing this piece out of the spiral darkness into the light: Susan, Katie, Ted, Elle and Burn Oberwager, Sisters at Santa Sabine Center, Susan Jordan and Ronnie Wong, Sue Smith and George Gallaugher, Frances Hayward and Jonathan Hubbell, John, Chrissy and Dan Bright, Melissa Farley, Darca Morgan and Denali Nicholson.

Thank you to Betsy and Alan Carpenter for saying so many years ago, "Come stay with us while you audit medical school!" thus anchoring this creation in my experience of anatomy and embryology.

Thank you to my beautiful clients who, willing to share intimate known and unknown secrets of bodies, emotions, thoughts, souls and soles, define my work and passion.

Thank you to the good doctors who taught and talked with me, sharing their knowledge dignantly and indignantly, always with a willing generosity of engagement: Jimmy Katzel and Robert Steinberg, Grace and Steve Liu, Patty Alessi, Gary DeCrona, Lani Kask, Benjamin Spock, Melissa Farley, Alan Carpenter, Mimi Doohan, Tisha Douthwaite, Larry Mathers, Susan Mathes, Marcia McDonald, Augie Hermann and Julio Kuperman, Linda Hopkins, Lee Vagt, Joel Alter and Cheri Quincy, John Knapp, Marcia Wiley-Stanley, Ted Wunderlick and Jerri Jo Idarius, Cal Seeba, Frances Barnes, Scott Anderson, Maria Nemeth, Carol Kohli, Caryn Levin-McCloskey, Victoria Jett, Laura Samartino, Valerie Luoto and Lucille Sanders, Regu Harichandran, Rajkumar Rehunathan and Sanju.

Thank you to my past and present collectives: Emma Goldman Clinic for Women and Hera, Iowa City, Iowa, Bay Area Radical Therapy and Issues in Radical Therapy, Round Mountain Cooperative Healing Center, and Mendocino Massage Therapy. Thank you H7Sisters, MAGG, and Blue Heron Swim Team.

Thank you New Dimensions Radio, Michael and Justine Willis Toms, The Flow Fund, PEO Chapter WQ, Resource Counseling Center, Philadelphia, Pennsylvania and Yoga Mendocino, Ukiah, California.

Thank you to Dover Publications, Inc., 180 Varick Street, New York, NY 10014 and Rudolf Koch, PhD, *The Book of Signs,* and LeRoy H. Appleton, *American Indian Design & Decoration.*

Thank you to my coaches: Frances Hayward, Arlene Goldbard, Kate Magruder, Meca Wawona, Nancy Roca, Linda Francis, Patti Campbell, Marilyn Katzel, Mary Paffard, Sheryl Green, Katie Gibbs, Skip Gibbs, Daphne Macneil, Elise Goothers, Guy Albert, Phyllis Webb, Susan Knopf, Peggy Agnew, Kathleen Bell, Joanie Springer, Joyce Patterson, Judith Page, Susan Pottish, Jana DePamphilis, Candice Becket and David Smith, Judy and Larry Ballenger, Yvonne Sligh, Susan Larkin, Susan Flint and Sandra Linn, Bill Walls, Larry Booth, Dede Parmley, Rebecca Campbell, Hogie Wyckoff, Jacque Cook and Deb Nye, Betty Aten, Dena Goplerud, Arlene Faulk, Nan Jones, Evelyn Thomas, Les Scher and Victor Fresquet, Tae Kim, LaSalle Whipple, Ishqa Hillman, Elizabeth Crow, Mindy Blumann, Anne Caviglia, Julia Schnitzler, and Jan Roemmick. Thank you Bill Staudenheimer, Peggy Ricketts, Tom Rogalsky and Victoria Donner. Thank you Fred Jordan, Craig and Kimberly Nicholson. And thank you to Bonnie Bell and David Todd, Patty Joslyn, Stephanie Hoppe and Joan Giannecchini and Miss Pickles, Steve Oliveria and David Bushway, Chris Pugh, Karl Bralich, Kirk Fuller, Robert Wills, and to you, my Forget-Me-Nots.

Thank you to Mrs. Kisses and Lorie Leaf, Mary X Gustafson and Carla DeCrona. Thank you all for your spacious hearts, good friendships and strong support. You are so fine. I did this with you.

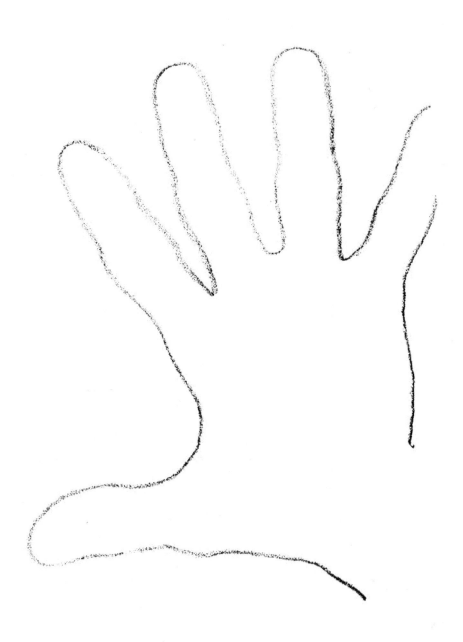

Introduction: Journey of a Lifetime

If we pursue a biological event or process, we discover that each element is part of a system and participates in multiple systems, that each of these systems interacts with all the others, that circularity of process is typical and the application of nice, tight logic leads us nowhere.

W. C. Ellerbroek, MD

Dear One,

Thank you for joining me. My intention in writing this book is to stoke the fires of beauty and health in women's bodies.

I am thankful to you for allowing me this opportunity to explore the question that has guided and animated my life's work: How do we practice appreciation and gratitude for these miraculous bodies?

Seeking answers, I will visit many topics: food and drink, movement and rest, thoughts and habits we infuse into our lives that can help support or destroy this absolutely amazing structure, our bodies.

Let me share with you what I know from over forty years of hands-on practice in massage, movement and meditation.

As companions, we embark on an exploration of a number of medical traditions. My premise is that good medicine is good medicine, regardless of origin.

My grandmother used to say, "I came to my senses and realized…" Later on she shortened it to "I came to…," implying an awareness that reliably produced solutions. Just so, this book is the product of a lifelong journey of "coming to my senses," my way of offering you advice that will make coming to your own senses both comfortable and exciting.

I want to live in a world permeated by adoration and respect for every one's body. Together, we can make these changes.

Having studied and practiced the science of what works for more than four decades, I have become the opposite of "clueless": to coin a word, I am clueful. I consider myself a doctor of what works, proficient at diagnostics, referral and suggestions. In saying that I diagnose, I use a term "owned" by the medical profession, thus risking being branded an outlaw. In the sixties, when I started practicing massage in the Midwest, massage was illegal. The very term was considered a code word for prostitution. At other times, medical professionals considered massage quackery.

But I am unwilling to surrender quietly. I know touch is capable of healing and I am intractable. I want massage to be massage without sexual connotations. I do not want to share even the name of my practice with exploiters and perpetrators.

Therapeutic massage is hands-on healing treatment for real maladies of mind, body and spirit, a fit companion to any medical treatment. Massage works by removing insults, by pacifying, restoring, relieving daily aches and pains. Simple, noninvasive diagnostic methods are possible through touch. Accompany me on my journey, share my secrets, and the quality of your life will improve. You will be able to address both internal and external conflicts. You will feel better. We will have a good time.

Let me tell you a true story. A gentleman had fallen from a

ladder, almost cutting himself in two. A year and a half later, he found himself in constant untreatable pain. He asked his physician, who worked at a large medical institution in California, "Will having a massage help?"

"No," said the doctor, "It won't help." Shrugging a shoulder, he dismissed the patient: "It will just feel good."

I have the utmost respect and appreciation for the very fallible science and practice of trauma medicine. I honor the league of women and men around the world practicing allopathic medicine. Every moment, twenty-four hours a day, 365 days a year, they work miracles. Some of my most valuable training came through auditing medical school classes.

But allopathy, our conventional medicine here in the United States, is only one valid form of healing. From study and experience, I am also respectful of other world medical traditions. My spectrum of world medical practices includes six traditions:

1. Allopathic Medicine or "Western" medicine, is the youngest medical tradition on this planet. As practiced in this country, it is deeply enmeshed with government funding, pharmaceutical and chemical businesses and insurance companies, so that economic considerations often trump other priorities. The greatest expertise of Allopathic medicine is physical trauma medicine, the type of lifesaving techniques practiced on television in "M.A.S.H.", "E.R." or "House." The most competent practitioners and greatest resources are often found in teaching hospitals or large city and county hospitals such as San Francisco General, New York City Bellevue or Cook County Hospital in Chicago. If you are injured in a war or car accident, the trauma unit offers the highest odds of surviving.

2. Indigenous Medicine exists in every culture, encompassing the largest and oldest traditions, some hidden to outsiders. Explore the daily life of any community and you will discover many healing traditions alive and well. Patience, respect and curiosity are required to unlock this treasure chest.

3. Siddha Vaidya (meaning subatomic medicine) and Ayurvedic Medicine, or Indian medicine, are the oldest continually practiced and documented medical disciplines.

Siddha Vaidya, from the Dravidian Civilization, Indus River Valley, 5000 BCE, still holds secret formulas for regenerating of sages and royalty. The Ayruvedic tradition, 2500 BCE, promoted by the Vedas shares much the same information in the areas of surgery, nutrition, pharmaceuticals, yoga (exercise, breathing and meditation), massage, astrology and other esoteric spokes of the healing wheel. From Siddha Vaidya and Ayurvedic teaching, it is easy to trace the next two medical traditions.

4. Chinese, aka Traditional Oriental, Medicine includes traditions of acupuncture and herbal medicines, well documented in Asia. The Chinese tradition is known to many through Buddhism and other Pacific Rim influences on the West. Acupuncture is the most integrated "alternative" medicine in contemporary Western medical tradition. Used for pain management, the "needles" also effectively treat substance addiction, particularly tobacco. The first acupuncture translation into a Romance language was by Girolano Cardono (1508-1576), an Italian physician and medical teacher from Milano.[1]

5. Unani Medicine, also called the "Tibb Method," is thought to have originated in Persia or Afghanistan. Unani medicine is almost as old, as complicated and as complete as the Siddha Vaidya and Ayurvedic traditions. It is difficult to get translations of the Unani teachings, but if the poetry of Hafiz and Rumi offer any indication of the sophisticated perspective on healing, I am eager to see Unani tradition translated into

Western languages. Study of Unani Tibb Method might be one of the ways we, as scholars and students of healing, can contribute to peace.

6. "Other Medicine" is my last loose grouping of world medical traditions, comprising many types of touch and healing. I prefer it to the terms "Alternative Medicine" and "Complementary Medicine." Most of what is practiced under the rubric "Alternative Medicine" is neither "alternative" nor is it "medicine." "Other" is the backbone supporting commonsense health practices often administered by masters or doctors, including several types of practitioners.

Chiropractors, bless their organized hearts, kept their tradition alive and well by banding together to be recognized by patients and insurance companies as viable options when a hitch in the git-along and other aches and pains demanded touch and movement as remedy. In the 1950's, chiropractors recognized the need for vitamins and minerals. Adjustments would not stay put if diet did not support healthy soft connective tissues.

Osteopaths, or Doctors of Osteopathy (DOs), are board certified by the allopathic system in all states in the United States and are granted the same status as medical doctors in dispensing pharmaceutical prescriptions, admitting patients to hospitals and ordering lab tests. A well-trained DO is capable of cracking a cold, reviving a liver or setting right a body smashed in a soft tissue accident. Naturopaths, certified in a few states, dispense "natural remedies." Massage therapists, certified in some states and licensed in others, have been vilified, even outlawed. There is a plethora of touch techniques named for their creators: Bowen, Pilates, Feldenkrais, Rosen, Rolfing, Alexander and Upledger to name a few.[2] Each of these practitioners has created a similar yet distinctive hands-on healing method.

So, when the gentleman in pain asked me, "Will a massage help?" The answer for him and 99.9% of the population is, "Yes. Absolutely." And ironically, "yes" is the answer for the very reason the man's doctor dismissed the practice. "It feels good."

What qualifies me to write this book? Simply: I write what I know. I am a student and a teacher. My grandmother was a healer with plants and poultices. My father, an artist, used touch when we ached. His back rubs always had a blessed ability to ease the flu, settle a cold, soothe sadness.

Until recently (and like so many women), my daily life made creative discipline nearly impossible. I felt I was doing well to eat greens, exercise three times a week, pay bills, clear my desk and be a mom. Often, at least one of these responsibilities overwhelmed me. So the discipline needed to focus on a book felt a long way off. I didn't have a conscious clue how to get to creative discipline, even when coached to "just write twenty minutes a day." Yeah, right.

Then, in the spring of 1996, I took my second Grand Canyon raft trip down the Colorado River. The second trip was a completion, a confirmation of my abilities. I had taken my first trip down the Colorado River twenty years earlier. The first trip, I recovered my balance. The second trip, I recovered my life.

The trips acted as bookends, bracketing two important decades in my life. At the conclusion of the second trip, my writing brain woke up. I had no choice but to write. For someone who loves to share and has always had a difficult time spelling, even speaking, writing has been an awakening. I experienced a geological shift in my being. For me, the act of writing proves to be an underpinning of my book: if I can complete this almost unimaginable task, *you* can accomplish whatever you have imagined to be impossible. *You* can accomplish your wildest dream.

First Journey, Grand Canyon, Colorado River, September 1976: Autumnal Equinox celebrated at Nankoeweap. High above the Anasazi mesquite orchards, I make the hike of my new life. The previous winter, in a cross-country skiing accident, I rotated my lower limb 360 degrees around my knee. By the grace of a gold wire, a steel staple and artwork by the best allopathic knee surgeon, seven months later I climb the narrow steep trail to the ancient granaries of the indigenous ancestors of the Hopi. As I climb, balance is my priority. Attention. Focus. Breath. Movement. Sensation. Pain. Rest. Placement. Release. Contact. Push. The dry, hot breeze cuts through centuries. Cellular memory floods my eyes, my blood, my heart. I tell myself to return to my body, breathing, expanding and contracting. Take everything gently: feel the ache, rub the knee. I know this place. I have looked over this valley before. I turn and slowly retrace the trail. Descending, I find it difficult to balance before pain overtakes the knee. In the gentle step up, light compression sends neurological information from the joints to the brain, giving my body more placement power and accuracy. Stepping down, I must put weight on my joint before I know my balance. It feels like following a recipe: carefully mix the water into the dry ingredients, blending slowly to avoid lumps. The step down this trail is lumpy. My antiquated brain must learn from a new knee before the full impact of weight is easily borne by my rearranged tissues.

Life imitates the Grand Canyon. Danger and beauty are married. Having safely descended and settled in at the river's edge, I gaze at brown lava foam that resembles giant soft sponges. But these rocks are hard enough to rip you or your raft apart in a New York second.

Life was born in the Grand Canyon. It may have been born in other places, too, but sitting here, I know I am touching the womb of the earth. Sacred, silent, savage, mighty, majestic and face-to-face with eternity in this moment, she'll take your breath away and give you peace. She stills your mind and scrambles your heart, lets you sleep quietly next to fire ants and nibbling mice, sucks you into a water hole hundreds of feet deep and gives you enough foam-trapped breathable air to stay conscious through the flush. She constantly forgives, scooping you out for another day. Yet she will take your life if it is time.

God lives in the Grand Canyon, in a billion years of time still mysterious to scientists. Bright angel shale, as high as a house, looks firm and solid, yet crumbles to sparkling dust in your hand. Beautiful mauve, deep sea green turquoise, true ochre - colors as smooth as the tranquil sea that laid these beds. Holiness escapes through your sounding voice in a rolling unstoppable "Ahhaaa."

Second Journey, Grand Canyon, Colorado River, March 1996. Why this second trip? My daughter had just turned 16. I had lived long enough to see her become a young woman. Whatever I had given her has taken root: secure, deep and everlasting. I hope as she grows, she will discover I have blessed her with gifts and treasures. But today they seemed darkly veiled by the contemporary American cultural norm of daughter against mother.

When my daughter was five, I had the opportunity to visit Nicaragua at war. It was an exciting invitation, an adventure that called to my spirit. But I felt it would not be a responsible move for the mom of a young one. I said, "Thank you very much; when my daughter is of age to lose her mom to worldly explorations, I'll start back on my wild woman expeditions." With her sixteenth birthday, I felt the time had come to begin my adventures again. On my first foray, I fell in love with a dashing guide on a nature cruise in Costa Rica. Then I need-ed an antidote to that fairy tale romance; although I'd put my emotions on hold, my imagination continued to replay roman-tic scenes. My grandmother used to say, "Pull yourself together, Honey." I thought a trip down the Colorado River might pull my unbalanced parts together, as it had twenty years before.

The universe opens a door. There was space for a massage therapist-bodyworker on a private raft trip planned by friends. I was in good health, a seasoned swimmer. I could do some work on the river to offset expenses. Still, I wavered. Then, a friend arrived with a story from *Life's Big Questions* by Jonathan Robinson.[3] "If you were guaranteed not to fail, what would you be doing?" Easy answer. "I would be working and traveling in the world. I've recovered from the shock of my daughter mov-ing away to school at fourteen. I'm footloose and fancy-free. It will cost less to be on this trip than to stay at home. I can do this."

I embarked on the journey with a carefree spirit. What I dis-covered was anything but carefree. By journey's end, I felt I had survived boot camp: a man-made flood; a helicopter assault; two raft flips into water fifty-two degrees Fahrenheit; difficult rescues; hepatitis in the side-canyons; scorpions; ratty rock tra-verses hundreds of feet above the canyon floor; dung- and car-cass-infested beaches; alcoholic, drug-addicted, power-wired, self-loathing, moody, complaining, Machiavellian, pathologi-cal, hypochondriac colleagues—and more.

"More" included an experience of being chilled to the core. I was on a "sweep raft" that had been outfitted to rescue people that was itself sucked deep into a hole. The kayaker who res-cued me put me on the shore and headed downstream to look after his sweetheart. I hiked the shoreline downstream look-ing for my companions until I ran out of shore. In my sec-ond involuntary swim of the morning, the hypothermic March water drained body temperature as I pulled myself hand over hand, grasping roots and branches, along a flooded beaver village. Finding myself on an island, I gathered strength for yet another unwanted dip in the Colorado water, covering two more bone-chilling miles. Finally by 10:30 that morning, all rescues were complete. My companions stripped me naked and dressed me in dry long underwear, outerwear and a full suit of windproof rain gear to bake in the ninety-five degree heat. I stopped talking.

Returning home, I started writing on a computer for the first time. Compared to a trip through the jaws of death, writing a book is a stroll in the park.

My "Coven." Years ago, I had the privilege to become a member of what I affectionately call "The Little Old Ladies Christian Coven." Even though many of us don't qualify as either little or old, I've always called us "little old ladies" because when I first joined, Mother said to me: "It might not mean much to you now, at eighteen, but as you get older, it will."

She was right.

The group is my "coven" because there is a secret and because we are all women. I say "Christian" because the Lord's Prayer is spoken aloud at the beginning of each meeting. Yet, in truth, most spiritual traditions are represented. The only requirement is to believe in the concept of God.

PEO (Philanthropic Educational Organization is the official legal name, but everyone uses the initials) was founded in 1869 in Iowa. Besides being an early feminist support group, this international organization raises money for educational scholarships. Over $100 million has been made from garage and bake sales and awarded to women all over the world who wish to pursue knowledge and attain skills. Spoken together at the opening of the meeting is a lovely affirmation in the language of the day:

The objects and aims of this sisterhood shall be general improvement, which shall comprehend more especially the following points:

To seek growth in charity toward all with whom we associate, and a just comprehension of and adherence to the qualities of Faith, Love, Purity, Justice and Truth.

To seek growth in knowledge and in culture and to obtain all possible wisdom from nature, art, books, study and society and to radiate all light possible by conversation, by writing and by the right exercise of any talents we possess. To aim at self-control, equipoise and symmetry of character and temperance in opinions, speech and habits.

It shall be the chief duty of each member to consider thoughtfully the full import of this sisterhood. This will include a sincere regard for our influence in the community, a careful consideration of feeling when speaking and a determination to do all we can at all times and under all circumstances to express a loving concern for each sister.

This lovely affirmation was written at Iowa Wesleyan College, Mt. Pleasant, Iowa in 1869 by a group of sixteen-, seventeen- and eighteen-year-old women—Mary Allen Stafford, Ella Stewart, Alice Bird Babb, Hatti Briggs Bousquet, Franc Roads Elliott, Alice Virginia Coffin and Suela Pearson Penfield. In the tradition of "expressing a loving concern for all sisters," I am honored to share with you my discoveries and my experiments as well as the profound teachings from my clients, friends and family.

BODY MATTERS explores our wisdom, our gifts and our responsibilities as twenty-first-century women.

The first three chapters focus on three sites, three places to

go in our bodies with added awareness: feet, diaphragms and belly. The next three chapters focus on behaviors or actions that create health: smiling, eating and listening. These are adventure stories, mysteries and visits to the twilight zone. Chapter 7 describes simple healing guidelines to integrate this information. Chapter 8 is titled "conclusion" but it seems/feels as if it is just a place to rest.

Be wise in the way you use the information in this book. Try things out and pay close attention to the effects on your unique body and spirit. My philosophy is to start with the least invasive, least expensive, most personal program. Health care does not cost so much when we do it ourselves. It behooves us to follow our grandmothers' advice: "an ounce of prevention is worth a pound of cure." Beauty and wisdom are the by-products. But pay attention to the information your body is sharing: do not continue a treatment if your symptoms tell you it is time to stop. Take the next step. Ask for help.

As you begin to read, please consider the following questions. You may wish to jot down your answers and return to them from time to time.

How do you want to feel good? What parts of your body do you not like? What parts of your body do you like? What parts of your body complain when you are tired? What parts of your body did you once abuse? Are you still abusing? How old will you be when you die? Close your eyes. Take a deep easy breath in and out. Listen. An age will appear to you. Are you satisfied? What kind of shape will you be in before you die? Is there anything that needs to change for you to feel satisfied with your answers?

You are closer to vibrant health than you ever imagined. Come with me: our journey has already started.

> *Love a little your body*
> *Seen in the dim morning mirror*
> *The woman cradled by sleep.*
> *Thinking, "How lovely you are this*
> *   day."*
> *Begin with gratitude.*

—DN
August 29, 2001

❀ ❀ ❀

Notes

1 Girolamo Cardano (1508-1576), a physician and medical teacher from Milano. Italy. "Chinese Acupuncture in Italy." *American Journal of Chinese Medicine*, Vol 2, 1974 p. 49–52.

2 Pilates, Feldenkrais, Rolfing, Alexander, Upledger, Rosen. See glossary for description of individual practitioner.

3 Jonathan Robinson, *Life's Big Questions*, Berkeley, CA: Conari Press, 2001. (previously published as *The Little Book of Big Questions*).

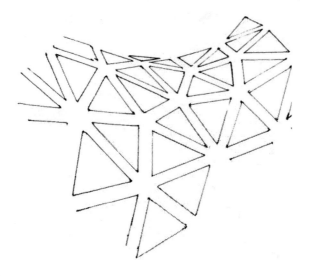

Illustration based on a view from inside a bubble.
– Science News, circa 2000.

1

Sole of Being

In the process of creating and designing humans, feet came first. Monday morning in Paradise found the Creator fresh from a fabulous vacation on the pristine beaches of the Yucatan. Pulling strands of golden thread from the spinning-wheel of the universe, the Creator spent almost all week building the feet. Then just three hours before the end of the work week and after way too much food and drink for lunch, the Creator returned to the studio Friday afternoon to design the knees. Not that major miracles cannot be accomplished in Heaven in a split second, mind you. But a full stomach and dicey food combinations affect the Creator just like the rest of us. Wanting to finish the human before the long weekend, the Creator put two bones together at the ankle, connecting them with a beautiful

crisscross sheath; slapped a couple of fat
"Cs" sideways; latched the thighbone and
set the trunk, head, arms and hands in
order on top. Fast, slick and, hey, the feet
could carry anything. Give the Creator
a break, it had been a spectacular week
and She needed a rest.

Feet are truly a wonder. Delicate bone placement, clever connections and a profound range of movement characterize their
amazing structure. These architectural masterpieces feature
arches on both the inside and the outside of the foot (medial
and lateral). Feet are capable of holding a thousand pounds on
one tiny point (such as stiletto heels), marching three times
around the equator of the earth in a lifetime (this is only the
average distance humans walk), dancing on the moon and
recovering each night from whatever abuse we've given them
during the day.

How can the body of this book start with feet? Because, as
my mother says, "When your feet hurt, everything hurts." She
is right. I was blessed with a mom who had "difficult to fit"
feet and grandparents who had enough sense to spend money
on shoes that actually fit her, so that "comfortable," the first
criterion for intelligent shoe-buying, was passed down to me
as if foot care were part of my genetic code. Caring for the feet
was as integral to daily life as eating, sleeping and brushing my
teeth. I love my feet. I always have.

**Great Teachers of the World Include Foot Care in
Their Texts.** Washing, then massaging the feet with olive oil
and essential oils, is common practice in the Bible: 500 times
someone is anointed with oil. I wonder if it's just a coincidence that the inventors of "soul" and "sole," "heal" and "heel"

assigned the same sounds to English words I use so often and prize so highly. Feet are the soul/sole connection to the rest of your being. We help all of ourselves by helping our feet. When asked, "What is the meaning of life?" a professor I know replied, "Connecting the heart and soul." I have to add connecting the heart and soul with the feet. In these human bodies, grounding and action move our feelings, sensibilities and essences into life. That's why Rabbi Abraham Joshua Heschel described demonstrating with Martin Luther King as "praying with our feet."

In the early seventies, while an undergraduate at the University of Iowa, I met a Mennonite woman, Edna King, practicing foot massage, sometimes called "Reflexology." For an hour each week, Edna worked on my feet until finally, after a year, she let me work on her feet. I was elated. Apprenticing to a master was and still is my education of choice.

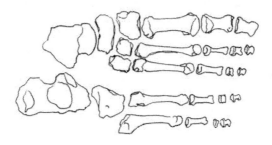

I soon had a facility from which to practice: The Emma Goldman Clinic for Women.[1] This women-owned and -run medical center was the haven where I began practicing massage and bodywork. In those years, massage and bodywork were often taken to mean prostitution and car repair. But in this feminist health collective, my work was respected as healing art. I worked to my heart's content.

The foot is composed of five layers of muscle and tissue, twenty-eight bones in an intricate five-arch structure, 24,000 nerve endings propelling incredibly complicated motions:

invert, evert, two-phase gait, 40 percent swing phase and 60 percent stance phase. From experience, we know a lot can go wrong with our feet. And when something does go wrong with our feet, just as with our hearts, life can be crippled.   At best, we ignore our feet and at worst we regularly abuse them. Hand-icapped by insufficient awareness of feet in their conventional medical training, doctors often collude with our ignorance and abuse. Indeed, at this time in biomedical technology, it is gen-erally safer to have heart repair, or hip or knee replacement sur-gery than surgery on our feet (or hands)! Ignorant experts plus injured consumers plus irreversible procedures too often equal a low success rate and persistent pain. My advice: for your feet, exhaust all avenues of treatment before consenting to surgery. Try exercise and yoga, diet and nutritional supplements, self-massage and professional reflexology, chiropractic and osteo-pathic adjustments, orthopedic and z-coil shoes, foot soaks and love poems before considering sur-gery as an option.

When Our Feet Are Healthy we stand with our toes and our heels in alignment, bearing weight evenly on each foot. But most of us do not wear our feet evenly. If you walk with your toes turned farther out than your heels, you habitually jam your lower back. If your heels are farther out than your toes as you walk, your body alignment produces a ballerina butt and compromised knees.

Look at your favorite shoes. Are both sides evenly worn? If the inside of your shoe is more worn than the outside, the arch on the inside "pronates" (that is, moves toward the ground), meaning you are flatfooted. It is likely that you are knock-kneed rather than bowlegged. Your base is too narrow. Fast-moving dogs might deck you by bumping the side of your knee, your inner thighs could chafe and you may need to wear diapers as your bladder complains of inadequate support. The fabulous muscles of the pelvic floor (together called the urogenital diaphragm) support your inside abdominal organs, which is much easier when your feet are properly aligned.

If the outside lateral edge of your shoe is worn more than the inside edge of the shoe, you may be prone to sprained ankles and "bad" knees, a sensitive lower back and aching hips.

In either case, the good news is that your feet have much more support to give. Not aligning them to your body is like having a savings account in your name and lacking the password! With the help of a yoga, meditation, or martial arts teacher and your own practice, balanced feet will make your energy flow.

Feet Face Other Challenges. Edema (swelling due to excess fluid retention) shows up around the feet and ankles. Cramps and muscle aches of the legs or feet have afflicted most of us sometime in our lives. Varicose veins emerge and can leave you feeling as if someone had started an unauthorized art project on your lower limbs.

If you have any of these problems, let me sing to you the praises of compression hose, an aid to the legs and feet. I never imagined that someone occasionally described as a flower child, hippie or new age feminist would champion tight-fitting socks! Generally, I hate tight-fitting clothes. But I do love being on the road to beautiful and healthy old ladyhood. Compression hose are the original support stockings. The medical design of these stockings is graduated compression, greatest at the ankle and gradually decreasing up the leg. This assists blood and lymphatic circulation. I thought compression hose went with varicose veins and thinning hair, but I was wrong. They are fabulous almost anywhere. Compression hose are the best medicine for airplane trips or long days of appointments. When I wear them, I am not as tired at the end of the day. I sleep better those nights because the lymph system has less cleanup and more "support" adjusting to changes in latitude, longitude and altitude. In Chapter 3, Buddha Full Belly, we will talk more about our lymph system.

One of my favorite doctors says, "Everyone over forty should put 'em on everyday." Compression hose are your ounce of prevention in addressing potential strokes, heart disease and lymphedema. While there is no way to prove this, I leap to suggest they may even be a factor in cancer prevention, since a healthy lymph system is the scavenger of toxins. Put them on before you get out of bed in the morning. This is when your legs are the most drained of lymph. The support should feel good. The sensation of compression reassures your whole system. If you do not immediately experience a sigh of relief—with your veins and lymphatics chorusing, "Yes!"—you have the wrong size or do not need this kind of support yet. My advice is to embrace them, as a generic remedy to aging, prevention of edema and support for circulation, before it is medically necessary for compression hose to embrace you. In ten years there will be designer compression hose as smart women create the need for fashion shades. But for now white, black and tan are the color choices. They come as dress or sport knee-hi or panty hose. When wearing pants, I choose the men's dress knee-hi for warmth and sturdiness.

Exercise for the Feet. Easy exercise is another necessary component of long-term relief for foot and leg cramps. Let me introduce you to yoga balls, known to some of us as rubber softball-sized pool and pet toys. So much happens when using these balls: warming, energizing and planting yourself in present time. They are bright, four inches in diameter, with a nubbly texture. I prefer mine to be squishy. Find these balls in pet and pool supply stores. The ideal ball is not too hard, not too soft, with enough texture to grip with your toes and feet. They serve us best in pairs.

Using the Balls. Do you sometimes feel uncertain about your balance? Once you focus on your feet, balance improves. Start playing with your feet while sitting in a chair. Feel your feet on the ground. Rock your feet inside, outside, all around the edges. Watch your feet move together and apart. Play dancing feet. Put tunes in your toes, ankles and knees. Pretend you are one of the Rockettes at New York's Radio City Music Hall. With friends or by yourself, use your imagination for two minutes, tucking, turning your feet in all possible and impossible positions. Smile at your amazing dancing feet, acting out while you are sitting down. After your two-minute foot exercise, cross your right leg over your left leg. Move your right foot in a clockwise circle. Move your right hand in a counterclockwise circle. Laugh. We are hard wired for symmetry and balance. Change leg crossing: left leg over right leg. Repeat.

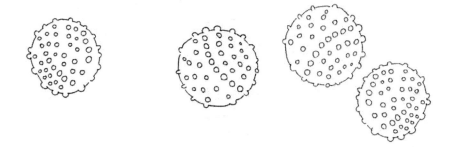

Stand with weight evenly on both feet. Feel yourself "standing on your own two feet." Rock gently back and forth. Exhale from your belly. Feel the center of gravity pass through your body as you move. Move gently sideways. Put a ball under the arch of one foot. (If it's more comfortable for you, you can do this seated, standing at the wall or supporting yourself on the back of a chair.) For one minute, roll back and forth over the ball, warming up your architectural wonder. Vary the speed: sometimes fast, sometimes slow. Please repeat with the other foot. Feel a difference between the first and the second foot?

Sit down again. Sole to sole, hold the ball in your inverted feet. With both feet, press the ball together. Move the ball back and forth on the outside edge of one foot. Change feet. Repeat. Feel your ankles warming with the motion. Reverse directions. Move the inside arch back and forth on the ball; knock knees, little toe up. Eversion. Play with the ball between your foot and the floor, enthusiastically squishing those sweet pads of fat and muscle. As we age, we lose fat on the bottoms of our feet. (And the palm of our hands!) Keeping your feet strong and flexible compensates for that loss of padding.

With this lovely two- to four-minute warm-up, notice your breathing deepen. By massaging your feet, a number of reflexes in the rest of your body are stimulated. With this investment in dancing feet, the rest of your day will be more balanced.

As you become familiar with the foot ball warm-up, explore your feet using two balls and both feet at the same time, moving first in the same direction and then in the opposite direction. Do this sitting in a chair. By exercising your feet, you exercise your brain and the rest of your body.

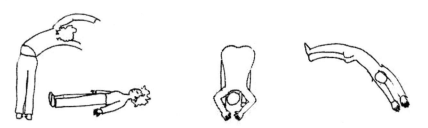

Exercise Without the Balls. Most of us are stuck in two or three body positions: sitting, standing and bending forward. Hampered by the resulting stiffness, we make tiny turns sideways, moving our whole torso instead of twisting around the spine. Even twisting is often easier on one side than the other. But this isn't how it needs to be. Regardless of age, we do best with a daily dose of all seven body positions. Humans are physically capable of standing, sitting, bending forward, bending backward, bending sideways, twisting or turning around the spine and being upside down. (Add walking both backward and forward to your daily routine and you've got nine steps to your best body, especially since walking backward often relieves sacral back pain.) All human movement encompasses these seven basic positions.

If you are getting too much of just a few of the seven positions, gentle exercise is needed to compensate for your limited movement. Let's say sitting is the position you occupy most of the time. For your feet and for your heart, here's a daily passive exercise which promotes healing in the sitting position: legs up the wall.

At the end of a workday, lie down on the floor perpendicular to a wall. Lie on your back, your head away from the wall. Put your legs up the wall in front of you. The comfortable distance between your bottom and the wall depends on your hamstrings, the back of your legs, so experiment to find your position. Your lower back should feel very comfortable resting easily on the floor. If there is a tiny window of light between your bottom and the floor, your butt is too close to the wall. Stay in your comfort zone. Do not push yourself toward the wall, thinking  a little stretch will help flexibility. It will not help. It will not hurt now, but later you will pay a price for not resting flat on the floor. Stay five minutes, collecting yourself from the busy day. Pretend your feet are crayons. Draw the alphabet, slowly and with intention as in penmanship class. Try both feet at the same time, mirroring each other. Write out the alphabet as fast as you can. Rest.

This is an inversion: part of you is upside down. Inversions are thought to alter hormone levels, thereby reducing brain arousal, blood pressure and fluid retention.[2] One mother I know takes afternoon time with her two-year-old daughter to put their legs up the wall. Together they share the stories of the day, enjoying this healing ritual. You will too. You will soon become addicted to this position, which allows you to reclaim the energy which

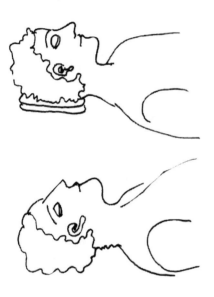

has become stuck from your body being in one position too long.

Use the foot balls in this inverted position. Put the balls on either side of your spine, deep in your butt, and rest for another five minutes. Be sure your forehead and your chin are equal distance from the floor. The back of your neck will not "jam" if you remember this guideline. Do not let "wrinkles" happen at the back of your neck. Lower your chin to your chest or place a towel under your head to slightly raise your head until your spine naturally elongates.

Move away from the wall by pulling your knees into your chest and rolling gently from side to side. Rest on your nondominant side. Push yourself up like a baby to a seated position. Stretch out again on your back, this time with extended legs. Put the balls under the widest part of your calves. Calves have an intimate relationship to the mind: it is hard to get either to quit working. Fat people have tight calves and so do skinny people. Relaxing the calves is a sophisticated body accomplishment. If you find this difficult, massaging your feet is a good place to begin relaxing the lower leg.

Let me plant a seed in your field of possibilities: what did you once do that you now think of as impossible? When I started writing this book, a handstand was impossible for me—even though I did handstands as a kid. It took me a long time to make being upside down a goal and then it took me more time to accomplish it. If I can do it, you can too! My organs appreciate it every time I go upside down. It makes me sleep better. There are a lot of ways to go upside down. The safest and most fun is slowly with supervision, strength building and support.

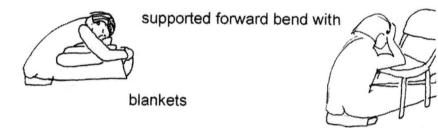

supported forward bend with

blankets

Long forward supported bends also make sleep come easier. Legs extended, firm pillows or neatly folded blankets on your lap, toes flexed, lean comfortably toward your toes with the mound supporting your insides, your trunk and your forehead for five minutes. Rest. Observe your breath. I also do a modified forward bend (no pillows) in the bathtub but this time, massaging my feet is the task.

One of the Loveliest Practices for our feet and our bodies is bathing. Foot baths are especially reviving. Twenty minutes with your tootsies tub side delivers a surprising impact. Organize the equipment, accessibly storing the props so you can take a break at a moment's notice. Soaking your feet is similar to the exercises described above which involve putting your feet up the wall, in that a brief respite can change the course of your day. Even on the best hair day ever, an extra five minutes of rest adds luster to your edges and peace to your core.

I recommend stocking the following supplies for a foot soak or a full-body immersion: a plastic dish tub for foot soaks; Epsom salts, a large box from the local pharmacy; powdered herbs and spices from the health food store: *bentonite, eucalyptus, wintergreen, witch hazel and cayenne.*

As some of these ingredients may be unfamiliar, let me explain how each one functions.

Bentonite. With a cleansing action like sea breezes or high mountain air, bentonite has the power to absorb positive ions. In the human body most toxins are positively charged. Bentonite is available as a pharmaceutical-grade, buff- or cream-colored powder usable internally as an intestinal cleanse. Bentonite is chemically structured as a broad flat card with a negative charge; its large surface acts as a sponge, gathering 800 times its weight in positively charged ions. Bentonite contains more than two dozen trace minerals, many essential for hormonal humming. Bentonite is very fine dust, so when you work with it, use one of the inexpensive dust masks available in hardware stores. You may want to do this mixing in the garage or outside, to avoid spreading dust. Be patient and stir thoroughly.

Eucalyptus is an antiseptic and disinfectant used as a relaxant. For eons, Australian First People used the leaves to cover wounds.

Wintergreen gives us oil of methyl salicylate, a relative of aspirin. Bathing with wintergreen leaves can relieve headaches, inflammations and joint pains.

Witch hazel, effective for hemorrhoids, heals skin irritations such as bites, stings, chafing and bruises.

Cayenne, used externally, stimulates surface circulation. If too much cayenne is present, tender tissue, such as the vaginal area, will feel stimulated beyond the comfort zone. Cayenne relieves local backaches, rheumatism, stiffness and headaches. It relaxes muscles and improves capillary tone.

To create a generous supply of this bath concoction, mix in the following proportions and keep on hand:

BENTONITE	2 CUPS
EPSOM SALTS	2 CUPS
EUCALYPTUS	1 CUP
WINTERGREEN	1 CUP
WITCH HAZEL	1 CUP
CAYENNE	1/8 CUP

This concoction was taught to me by a shaman who considered thoughts to be tangible ingredients. As you mix your own foot-soak formula, stir in healing thoughts. When you soak, the prayers and blessing you stirred into your concoction will return to bless you. While you are soaking, please bless the rest of us too!

When you're ready for a soak, shake a quarter cup of this

mixture with two cups of water in a lidded jar, then add the resulting soup to your tub. To top off this formula, I add a therapeutic-grade essential oil, the choice depending on my mood. If I am making up a small gift package of the concoction, I use five to ten drops of lemon or lavender oil to one and one-half cups of the mixture. To soothe menopausal grumpiness, five drops of clary sage and rosewood oil in the tub lightens my spirits. You are you own best physician. You are your own best nose, so choose the smells which suit you best.

Please note that the herbal concoction turns the water brown. Years ago, a young friend observing my tub water commented to her mother that Darca certainly was dirty!

If you don't have time to mix up this concoction, you will enjoy a bath with two to four cups of Epsom salts. Add a quarter cup of bentonite (mix the powder with water in a lidded jar first) and five drops of therapeutic-grade essential oil. Candlelight or not, hang out for twenty minutes drinking in the quiet, admiring your limbs, gratitude bathing every cell.

If your water is chlorinated, add sodium thiosulphate, a fish tank dechlorinator, to your bath. Just as this valuable chemical "protects your fish from agony or death," it will prevent your skin from absorbing toxic chlorine which so easily damages the

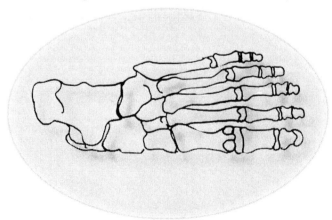

endocrine system, especially the thyroid gland. An unhappy thyroid shows up as fatigue, hair loss, extreme weight gain or loss and countless other symptoms. Use thirty drops for a full bathtub, two drops for a sink full of water and one drop in a plastic dish tub. I keep a dropper bottle of sodium thiosulphate in my travel kit and another by my tub in a well-marked recycled plastic shampoo bottle with a pop-top lid for easy access. I use *DeChlor* dechlorinator "instant": one pint costs $7.35 at my local pet store. The label reads: "Sodium thiosulphate + chlorine = sodium chloride (salt). Use to remove chloramine: 2 drops per gallon chlorine and chlorine dioxide: 1 drop per 2 gallons."

When I have a client coming in for help with her overworked muscles, I ask her to soak for twenty minutes beforehand in a warm tub with two to four cups of Epsom salts. Between appointments on long workdays, I soak my feet for twenty minutes in warm water, adding 1/3 cup Epsom salts and 1/4 cup of the shaman's concoction of herbs and minerals.

When you're soaking, relax and avoid distractions. I finally broke my habit of letting work intrude on my sacred bathing space when I dropped the phone into the bathtub. I took that as a message from the water goddess. She demanded respect for her healing power. However, if it takes phones, calendars and lists to get you into the tub, start where you are. Sit and breathe with your hands palm up, as if you were resting. Let your fingers rest in their gentle natural curves. Maybe by the time the phone rings, you will no longer feel like answering it.

Toes Love to be Touched. In your warm tub, take hold of each toe in turn. Starting with the toe that has the most stories (the longest, the shortest, the most gnarled), massage all the way around each toe, being careful to touch everywhere! Begin on the tip and get into the base. Separate the toes, spreading them wide apart. Gently pull each toe. Give each toe a slight twist to the left, slight twist to the right. Massage the base of the nail and the skin. Nails are the outgrowth of bone. What a clever design, protecting the ends of our appendages! I call this a little piggy practice for feet with soul. As you massage, appreciate these marvelous structures. Talk out loud to them, even if you start with "This little piggy went to…." what market? Where in the world have your little piggies taken you?

Bend your knee to access your foot. Using both hands, enfold the toes and the body of the foot. Hold your foot so the joints feel encased. Slightly squeeze your foot. Joints love to be supported. With delicate and direct pressure, push your toes into the natural nest of the joints. Align your movement with the natural structure of the foot, even if it looks deformed to you. This movement is not a flexion or a bending of the toes. Be gentle. Be firm. Your foot is the director. Your hands are following foot and toe directions. Each toe wants individualized attention. Holding the great toe with your fingers, push it into your foot with gentle pressure. This should not be abrupt or require a lot of pressure. It should be precise, directly angled into the joint, no twisting or turning. It could make you inhale deeply and exhale with a sigh of relief. Gentle joint compression delivers a time out, a no-penalty gift to your nervous system. Practice joint support on your friends. Teach them how to do it to you. Sharing is the best way to get joint support! If we share, we can have everything we need and want.

As you massage your feet, listen with your touch to the sounds and sensations of your toes. Sore spots and calluses are clues to nutritional, mechanical and structural glitches in your mental, emotional, physical and spiritual life. I believe calluses are warnings. If you have a callus on the outside of your little toe, your hearing might be compromised. If there is a callus on the ball of your foot, your heart might have calcium hanging out too close to the valves. This is a red flag. Get into your garden and eat those dark green, leafy veggies as if your life depended on it—almost more than anyone knows.

Cleaning up your calluses and sore spots are like cleaning up a polluted river. Even one massage makes a difference, especially when one massage follows another and another. When you start again each day with willingness and intention, all sorts of miracles occur. As you continue the foot soaks and massaging, you will notice some sore places never return. Who you were years ago is not who you are today. The story goes that ninety-eight percent of the atoms present in our body today will be replaced by new atoms within the year! It is our ideas, our constructed realities that stay the same! Scars depart as we integrate ourselves into present time. As we are lengthening in yoga class, one of my favorite lines is, "Our bodies are plastic, it is our brains that are set in cement!"

Plantar Warts. Do you have plantar warts on your feet? They are those little hard spots that grow and spread, looking as if there are "seeds" in the center. Here's a home remedy: For an hour run water as hot as you can stand over the plantar wart. At the end of the hour, take a good pair of tweezers to the middle of the unwanted guest and pluck it out. Rub a pumice stone over the remaining tough skin your smart body built up as a defense to contain the invading wart. This slick trick often excises small plantar warts completely. The larger ones might need this treatment several times. After treatment, apply therapeutic-grade essential oil of clove or oregano to plantar warts to suffocate any lingering intruders.

Most of Us Are Made to Our Own Measure. You are taller or shorter, thinner or wider than I am, but our ratios are the same. You have a personal body unit measurement, your own unique "inch": it's the distance between the first and second bend of your pointer finger. The measurement is from the first joint below your fingernail to the next joint of the finger

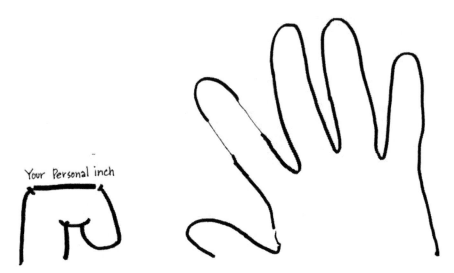

Your Personal inch

(distal—far away, to proximal— close by.) Fix this information in your mind. Measured with this personal inch, you most likely cover twelve "inches" from the inside bend at your elbow to the bend in your wrist; sixteen "inches" from your ankle to your knee; and twenty "inches" from your knee to the top of your femur. Eight "inches" is the distance from your sixth rib to your waist and five "inches" from your waist to the femur (hipbone). Bear this in mind as we continue on our journey, as we will later use this measurement in other places on your body. Try this practical application of your personal inch. Attend to the second "inch" above the ankle on the inside of your leg. Press firmly around this area. For 99% of us, this point, a vortex of three meridians, kidney, liver, spleen, will be sensitive. Massaging at this point, called Sanyinjiao in Chinese acupuncture, helps

2 personal inch

personal inch

ANKLE BONE

MEDIAL MALLEOLUS

tenderness disappear. Return regularly to massage Sanyinjiao for general health maintenance and specific support for kidney, liver, spleen.

Therapeutic-Grade Essential Oils on Your Feet. Historically, essential oils were extracts of flora and fauna (musk oil). Therapeutic-grade essential oils meet an international standard for purity that requires them to be free from additives and adulterants. Using therapeutic-grade essential oil concentrates the healing power and scent of the plant or flower in liquid form. In combination with other healing practices, aromatics calm or excite, balance or protect us. Application of a therapeutic-grade essential oil on the feet is usually a safe way to send healing to other places in your body. There are many books and charts on essential oils.[3] Do your homework. This is an area of discussion and dissent. (Common to the human condition!) Essential oils can be toxic. Remember: that which is capable of healing is also capable of harming. Essential oils have a long lineage. Four thousand years ago, the Egyptians developed sophisticated extraction processes not yet matched by our technology. Today, you can order a therapeutic grade essential formula called Valor, based on a formula found in the British Museum and used in battle by Greek and Roman soldiers for courage. A nighttime application of Valor—the chiropractor in a bottle—seems to melt stiffness from my spine and soothes aching feet and legs. Several quality oil sources are listed in the chapter notes.[4]

Toenails. Trim your nails to suit the shape of your toes. Contrary to what you might have learned in hygiene class, my advice is not to trim your nails straight across. The other day, I did a yoga practice with two of my best friends. We all had our legs up the wall. Beautiful toenail polish decorating the tips of their lovely feet, both yoginis had nails shaped to the dimension of their toe tips. Graceful lines, integrated curves. This toenail style is good for protection of the bone, good for protection of the tissue and good for the health of the nail.

If your nail is thick or clouded, you, like 50 percent of the population, probably have onychomycosis, from *tinea unguium*, a fungus. Fungus is mad for you, eating you up. I believe it finds you irresistible because there is too much sugar in your diet. Natural fruit and juices, grains, breads and pastries, alcohol and sodas all count as sugar, so far as your body is concerned. Until recently, if you took an allopathic medication for foot fungus (also called ringworm of the nail), your toenails might clear up but you had to regularly check your blood to be sure the medication was not causing liver damage. In the past few years "Lamisil," a prescription antifungal medication, has been on the market. As with all pharmaceuticals, there are side effects for some people, but blood monitoring is no longer needed. Lamisil is effective on most skin fungus and therefore relieves the lymphatic system, the first line of defense against fungus. On clients who have finished the three-month course of medication, I have seen various aggravations on the skin slide off with a massage and application of therapeutic grade essential oils. Check with your prescribing physician.

Less expensive products with fewer side effects have recently appeared on the market. It is interesting to note the number of solutions for tinea unguium. Dr. Versendaal, chiropractor, says, "Vicks Vapo-Rub is the ticket." Mildred Jackson says the treatment for fungus is campho-phenique powder.[5] The essential oil of choice from Australia is tea tree oil or melaleuca. A therapeutic-grade formula called Purification, a blend of citronella (the aroma in bug candles), lemongrass, lavender and melaleuca, is also reported to be effective. Others use thyme essential oil. An over-the-counter product, Dr. G's, is reported to be a powerful antifungal. Sometimes a naturopathic treatment prescribed for one condition turns out to be good for another ailment. Some years ago the therapeutic treatment for radiation detoxification was soaking in hot water with a cup (yes, eight ounces) of bleach. I am not certain about soaks in chlorinated water for radiation detoxification, but I am certain soaks in chlorine bleach and water do kill fungus of the nail bed. In any case, like most out-of-balance body situations, diligence and discipline in applying formulas are keys to success.

Fungus on our bodies is decomposition before the cessation of the breath. Not good. The ability to decompose is the last of the life energies described in Ayurveda, one of India's healing traditions. "*Dhanam-java*" (Sanskrit for "wealthy conquest") is the life energy responsible for the disintegration of the dead body. We do not want virus, bacteria, parasites and fungus robbing the bank before our gifts have been shared with the world!

More Fascinating Foot Lore. Remember the "moons" on your fingernails and toenails that you asked your mother about years ago? The Chinese say big moons, or lunas, are the sign of long life. Strong, bright lunas are the sign of a healthy body. My lunas brighten up as I exercise more, breathe better and enjoy deep sleep. If I abuse my body, the lunas start to fade into the nail bed. Whether bright or fading, I have less moon on each toe and finger than I did as a child. My friends that have passed on showed me their leaving times through their fingernails. The ones with long life, who passed on in their sleep, had "setting moons": the moon literally "sets," disappearing behind the horizon of the cuticle. My friends who have danced with disease had "fading moons." The lunas remained in the sky of the nail bed but faded into the background. Then again, nothing is certain: I have another friend who has been perking along with no moons at all for at least twenty years.

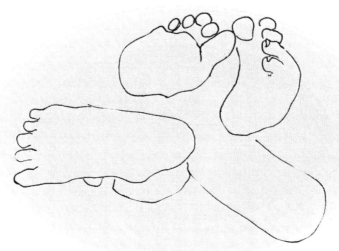

Her moons disappeared when she improved her diet and treated her fungal infections!

"Warm feet, cool head" is a Chinese prescription for a long and prosperous life. Most of us are interested in warming up our feet. How? Radiant sleep partners—spouses, lovers, dogs and cats as well as socks, electric blankets, hot water bottles, microwave corn bags and buckwheat hull pillows—can help. My tried-and-true story of the fail-safe foot-warming method bears repeating, particularly because it took me years to talk about it out loud.

You need a warm water source, a toilet and a large plastic cup, like the ones that come from fast food chains. In the bathroom before retiring, fill the container to the brim with warm water. Temperature is very important. It should be the temperature you want your feet to be. Either too hot or too cold will wreck havoc with your whole body thermostat. (If you have hot feet, you can use this method too, substituting cool water.) Sit on the toilet. Pour the water over your labia, the lips that protect the vagina and the urethra. You will immediately feel warming inside of your feet if you are using warm water and cooling if you are using cool water. In anatomical terms, you have just poured water over the pudendum, Latin for "area to be ashamed of," thus named by Christian monks in 500 AD.

Does it work for you? You have to try it to find out. Even today, I work with lovely, independent, powerful women who cannot pour warm water over their labia to treat their cold feet. Fifteen hundred years later, others still control our comfort zones! How can this be? In 1996, I had a conversation with the Chair of the International Committee on Medical Anatomy about changing the name of the pudenda to a more appropriate

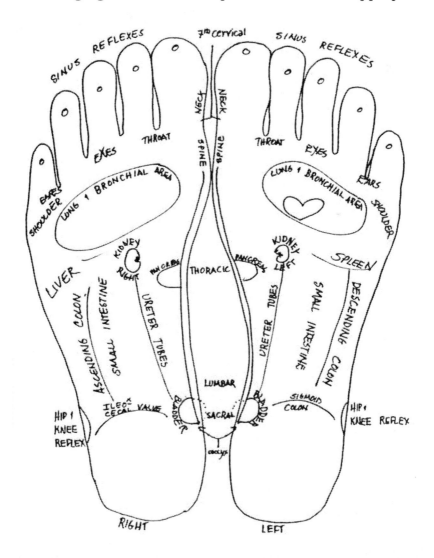

description. Almost all the muscles are named by their action. "External female genital" works. He was appalled. "It doesn't really mean area to be ashamed of, not anymore," he said with a cough and a sputter.

It took me more than ten years to regularly suggest to my clients this warm water treatment for cold feet. Evidently, the monks had a grip on my throat too. But this is the age of open secrets, so I invite you to share this one with everyone you know.

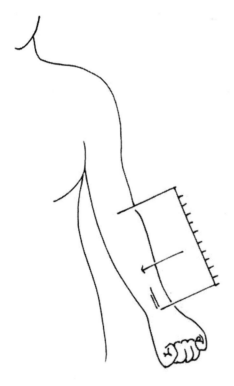

Cramping in the Feet or Calves (or anywhere else)! Yikes! If you have had cramps, you know how unpleasant they can be. The best immediate treatment comes from acupressure. On the inside of the arm opposite to the cramping foot (or leg), spread your hand from the center of the inside wrist bend to the bend in the elbow. This distance is your 12 personal inches. Earlier I showed you your personal inch as the distance between the first and second joints of the pointer finger. Now you have your personal foot. Halfway between the bend in your wrist and the bend in the elbow is six personal inches. From that spot, move one personal inch toward the wrist, distal. You are now five personal inches from the bend in the wrist. Flex your fist. The inward motion will raise the tendons in your arm. Between those tendons, press deep into the five-inch point. Hold that point until the cramp releases. This pressure is strong; the release in the cramping muscle should be immediate. Practice this before cramps strike.

My friend who suffered from terrible night leg cramps uses this technique. It has changed her sleep life. She used to be awakened nightly by severe leg cramps. After dealing with the cramping, she then had to lie awake solving the problems of her world for an hour before she could fall back to sleep. The first night she tried the acupressure reflex, she never emerged completely from her dreams, instead integrating her dreams with the act of applying deep pressure to the opposite arm at the five-inch point. She's a fast learner and deeply thankful to be freed from nighttime chatter.

Foot Pain. Do your feet ever hurt when you step out of bed in the morning? Pains in your feet upon arising often mean you are not getting the nutritional support your body needs. Long-term foot and leg cramps often leave when you balance calcium and other mineral absorption. Eating enough "good" fat also contributes to happy morning feet. (Chapter 4, Eating, includes a discussion on fats.) This is not merely a question of calcium intake. *Perfect Bones* by Pamela Levine has an extensive discussion of calcium.[6]

Let me give you the short version: over-the-counter antacids, used by many of us as a source of calcium carbonate (the calcium best used by muscles) is a scam. The stomach needs hydrochloric acid to absorb the calcium, not an antacid. Calcium carbonate would probably be usable without the antacid, but with it, calcium will likely be deposited in other areas of the body instead of the muscles. Inappropriate and unbecoming areas of deposit include the teeth, causing gum disease, which is really a form of arthritis, as teeth are bones. Calcium deposits on the delicate hairs and follicles of the inner ear sometimes cause hearing loss. They can also create stiffness in the structure of the eyeballs, impairing the ability of the eye to focus.

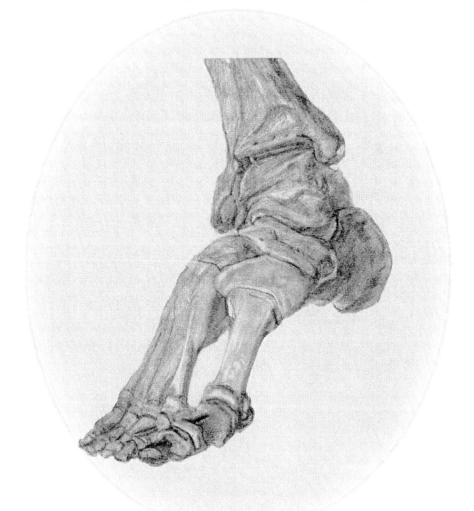

Marilyn Katzel

Other sites of inappropriate calcification include heel spurs and joint impingements. Another site of inappropriate calcification is the kidney and the formation of kidney stones. The list goes on and on.

Correct calcium guidelines come straight out of our bodies. Be vigilant. The amount of calcium we need changes. Calcium is a primary player in at least a dozen health-related situations. For instance, if you pass blood clots with your period, you might be calcium-deficient. Calcium is needed to coagulate the blood, make and keep teeth and bones strong, deliver babies, contract the heart, regulate temperature, keep blood pressure stable, lower cholesterol, maintain the pH balance of the blood, support the kidneys, support stomach acid and fight viruses. Calcium plays in the incredibly complex dimensions of acid-alkaline balance, a different percentage in almost every organ of our bodies! Oxygen and water keep us alive. Calcium keeps us running smoothly.

Therapeutic Treatment for the Feet. As I've made clear, feet were and still are one of my favorite body sites. Feet sing and sigh. Sometimes they tell me things allopathic tests take months to uncover. Often I work twenty minutes on each foot, interviewing my client, hearing stories stored in toes, feet, lower limbs and the rest of my client's body and soul. There are many foot stories. I want to share a few of them with you now.

You will gather your own foot stories as you start to touch your feet regularly. Remember, there is no such thing as a bad foot massage. Touch yourself with focus. Touch your friend with the same focus and a smile. Whatever else you do, you are manufacturing beauty and health by raising hormone levels of oxytocin, the hormone of tending and befriending. Oxytocin, one of the most important discoveries of the century, may hold the key to peace. Instead of flight or fight, oxytocin promotes cooperation and discussion about solutions. I believe this is the chemical of diplomacy. Oxytocin, also known as the hormone of love and cuddles, is responsible for the many proposals I have received after completing foot massages.

Practice on yourself and your dear ones: foot massage is an incredible gift for all ages. When I first began practicing, I wanted to share with everybody, especially those I dearly loved. I had gone off to college, joining the sixties' swing into protest and demonstration. Returning for a long summer visit to my hometown, I knew the farm and the cottage were important stops. As usual, Sunday was Lake Day. Grandpa ran the flag up. Grandma fried chicken. Mother baked pies and my aunt prepared fabulous seven-layer salad. The day had all the flavors of summer plus gorgeous weather. Grandpa, sitting in his mother-in-law's overstuffed rocker with coffee cup and saucer by his side, listening to church on the radio, was a perfect target for my newly developed expertise. But he wouldn't let me!

My dear grandfather, being from the old school, was not about to take his shoes off for any public display of skin. I bugged him, sat down on a little stool beside his feet, but they remained firmly planted on the floor, so I gave up. Mother intervened, "Now Dad, let her work on your feet. You'll like it." I had never heard anyone tell Grandpa what to do when he had not asked for advice. Happily starting out on the right foot, I oiled him up and methodically inched my way around every nook and cranny of that wonderful old foot. After twenty minutes, I pulled my fingers off his toes and asked, "There, shall I stop now?" "Ha!" he said, "You finish what you start! Don't want to be lopsided!"

Every time I returned home, Grandpa happily took off his shoes and socks for a treatment. Years later, he suffered a stroke. The next time I saw him, his right great toe was very tender around the tip. It made him jump when I touched it. This was new. His tender toe and feet taught me the truth about strokes:

the great toe is the reflex to the head, the whole head. The nail bed seems to be related to the face.

A few years ago, I treated another stroke victim. She was staying with her doctor friends in the mountains. As I worked on her feet out on their deck, the surgeon observed. Finding the tenderness to be midway outside of the left great toe, I surmised the arterial clot to be on the right side of her skull, just over the right ear. His fingers walked over his head collaborating my information, rubbing the right parietal section of his skull. "Yes. Here."

Right toe relates to left side of head. Left toe relates to right side of head. Body information stays on the same side of the foot, that is right shoulder, right foot. This is not rocket science: the information stored in our bodies informs the art and science of medical practice throughout the world.

Housing the Feet. Take your shoes off on a warm sandy beach. Dig your toes into the clean, tiny balls of silica. Buff your heels as you walk toward the pebble beach. Notice how slightly larger smooth rocks push on spots you don't normally feel when you slip on a shoe molded to your foot. As you walk, you are waking up your nerve endings, which faithfully support you. Try a barefoot walk in the grass. Has it really been so long since the sole of your foot felt the skin of Mother Earth? Kiss her skin with your bare sole. She needs you. You need her.

Women working as prostitutes cannot walk barefoot on the beach because their back legs have shortened from wearing the requisite spike heels. Despite having no connection with that oppression, neither of my grandmothers could walk barefoot on a beach either. Both of them had to wear shoes with heels because their legs cramped without the support heels provided to shortened gastrocnemius muscles. They had to wear heels, even on their slippers, to keep the pain away! Now I know how to release the closed-circuit neuromuscular loop between the brain and the lower leg, the whole leg and the hip. When I walk on a city street observing women hobbled by too-high heels, I think the physical and mental energy required to keep those muscles shortened, if released, would move mountains and change worlds. It is hard to find a better illustration of the price we pay for closed minds and crippled bodies. Why are we so committed to such a harmful practice?

Who proclaimed high heels make your calves look sexy? They are painful and hobbling and will kill you if ever you try to flee from rapists or terrorists. When I turned forty, my sister-in-law tried "high heels make your legs look sexy" on me. My calves, in any state, never look sexy. With my genetic inheritance, I am happy to sport thick tubes much like my greatgrandmother's lower limbs. They serve me well over hill and dale. My dear sister-in-law's comment, while well intended, was meant to bring me up to fashion standards. But it was impossible to wrap my mind around the concept! Or my feet into high-heeled ships, which slide my toes forward, lock my knees, and put my pelvic floor into a fun-house tilt. Torture. Give me baby dinosaur booties or Z-coil shoes, as long as they are comfortable. Let's give the high heels back to the men who invented them. Do you know the old riddle? Who was the most talented performer, Ginger Rogers or Fred Astaire? Hands down or feet first, Ginger Rogers. Everything Astaire did, she did backward and in high heels!

Trauma to the Feet. Aside from our minds, no other part of the body has been as systematically terrorized as our feet. Around the world and through the ages, cultures are characterized by how they treat the feet. China has a long history of binding upper-class girls' toes under the foot, stunting growth and destroying the ability to run or labor. Only in the Tang Dynasty, approximately 600 to 900 AD, were women released from foot slavery. It is no coincidence that the Tang Dynasty produced the most exquisite poetry and art created by both women and men in all of China's long history. Slave owners of the Americas routinely shackled slaves' anklebones. The best-forged chain in Georgia rendered a person a perpetual prisoner. This form of torture was horrifically well thought out. It did not serve the slave owner to disable the servant. Physiologically and psychologically, the ring around the ankles placed the essence and presence of a human being deep into captivity.

Kiss your feet. Be grateful they are free. Blow them smooches or plant a kiss squarely on the great toe. Bless your body and leap into consciousness. Consider this: the day is coming when healing schools will pull everything we know about healing together, leaning on the knowledge of all the world's tribes. Technical advancement will flourish side by side with healing chi, fantastically advanced lab tests with foot massage consultation, stethoscopes surrounded by prayer, appropriate intervention balanced with palliative care that respects the end of life.

Good medicine is always good medicine, regardless of its origins. Know that, and you're on solid footing.

❁ ❁ ❁

Notes

1 Emma Goldman Clinic for Women, 227 North Dubuque Street, Iowa City, Iowa 52240 319.337.2111 or 800.848.7684 www.emmagoldman@com

2 Roger Cole, PhD, University of California, San Diego, CA.

e-mail conversation, May 12, 2006. www.yogadelmar.com/rogercole for more infomation.

3 E. Joy Bowles, *Basic Chemistry of Aromatherapeutic Oils*. 3rd ed., St. Leonards, NSW, Australia: Allen & Unwin, 2003.

E. Joy Bowles, *A-Z Essential Oils: What They Are, Where They Come From. How They Work*. Hauppauge, NY: Barron's Educational Series, 2003.

Kurt Schnaubelt, PhD, *Medical Aromatherapy: Healing With Essential Oils*, Berkeley, CA: Frog Ltd, 1999.

Kurt Schnaubelt, PhD, *Advanced Aromatherapy: The Science of Essential Oil Therapy*, Rochester, VT: Healing Arts Press, 1998.

Daniel Penoel, MD and Rose-Marie Penoel, *Natural Home Health Care Using Essential Oils*, Orem, UT: Essential Science Publishing, 1998.

4 Sources for essential oils.

Bonnie Bell Gold, Custom blends made from high quality essential oils. bonnie@gaiastarworld.com. 707.467.0109

Elise Gootherts, egooth@gmail.com

Floracopeia, 206 Sacramento Street, Ste. 304, Nevada City, CA. 95959 www.floracopeia.com 530.470.9269

Jude LaBarre, judelabarre@sbcglobal.net 510.549.3393

Mindy Blumman, mindbl@yahoo.com 707.468.8658

5 Mildred Jackson, ND & Terri Teagued, *Handbook of Alternatives to Chemical Medicine,* Oakland, CA: Lawton-Teague Publications, 1975, p. 106.

6 Pamela Levine, RN, *Perfect Bones,* Ukiah, CA: The Nourishing Company, 2000.

2

The Body's Diaphragms: Life's Vibrant Trampolines

The health of diaphragms is a major support for agelessness. Healthy diaphragms are the springboard of youth. Know where your diaphragms are, how they work and how to keep them tuned. Listening to their language brings balance.

Diaphragms deliver general health information as well as information specific to each of the four areas they support:

> *The pelvic diaphragm, located between your pubic bone and "tailbone" or coccyx, holds the belly up and in and reports on fatigue.*
>
> *The thoracic diaphragm, the one most commonly referred to as the diaphragm, without modifier, is the muscle that moves your breath, changing form during fear and flight, action and restoration.*
>
> *The jaw diaphragm, the anchor for your tongue, energetically connects to the pelvic diaphragm: tense or tight jaw means tight or tense hips.*
>
> *The soft palatal diaphragm, the roof of your mouth, separates the intake of breath from the intake of food.*

Diaphragm, from the Greek, means "partition." In a moment of movement, your lungs and thoracic diaphragm create vacant space for the world to rush in. As the diaphragm contracts, shortening into the abdomen and pushing the stomach out, a vacuum is created in the already low pressured lungs and pleural cavity. Low pressure in the lungs allows air to rush in without effort. Like all large muscles, the diaphragm is one of the structures absorbing the overflow of tension from the rest of your body.

To experience these directly, touch the roof of your mouth with your tongue, move the tip of your tongue as if you were scratching the back of your throat. That is the soft palate. Now, with your hand, touch the skin under your chin, the lower jaw diaphragm. Then touch inside your mouth, under your tongue. This is the top of your lower jaw diaphragm. On an exhale, use your hands to feel the movement under your front ribs. This is the thoracic diaphragm. Touch between your tailbone and your pubic bone. This is your floor, the pelvic diaphragm.

All of these areas are trampolines. They grow tired when their riggings are crooked, unhinged, off track, overworked, under-rested or jammed with unspoken emotions.

The pelvic diaphragm is often where sagging begins. Old age sags. In this chapter, I'll share some ways to avoid sagging and recover from sagging if it happens. I want to start with a story of terminal sag.

In a medical school anatomy laboratory in 1996, I assisted with two dissections and observed dissection of twenty other cadavers. One man was quite barrel—chested, his bottom rib cage flaring. Opening the chest of this cadaver was the first physical procedure of the fall medical school class. Following the proper sequence, we peeled back skin and identified muscle, moving beyond the pectoralis major and minor to see bone webbed with intercostal muscle. In this procedure, the first cut is around the perimeter of the chest.

It is usually an easy lift to open up the thorax cavity, as if bones were fine wood and we were delicate carpenters using high-speed saws. But while other cadavers released their chest plates cooperatively, this rib lid—the front of the man's barrel chest—didn't budge. Finally, when we used a tool like a crowbar, the sternum and ribs reluctantly parted, opening the door to lungs and heart with loud cracking sounds.

Who says the dead do not speak? This tough old man told me a thousand stories. I thank him and everyone else who offers their earthly vessels for the education of our medical students.

The fibrous connective tissues on the underside of this man's rib lid looked like a century's worth of cobwebs in the corner of an abandoned barn. Crisscrossing fibers, pulled away by our efforts to see inside, stood like fine strands of hair, rigid with electricity. As in death, in life this poor man had no movement in his chest. He had been glued shut by his own juices.

It is standard procedure in anatomy labs that cadavers come without medical records. One usually knows the cause of death, but in this case we knew nothing. He had a staple in a heart valve from previous surgery, and a tiny clear plastic tube running through his neck to his navel. The small intestines were distended three times the normal size for six or seven inches in the lower right quadrant. In the medial posterior intestine, a few inches of colon barely the diameter of a little finger provided for passage of waste. A colon of extremes: distention and constriction.

If I could have helped this man during his lifetime, my treatments of choice—the least invasive, most economical and medically profound—would have been castor oil packs, gentle massage and breathing exercises. Castor oil packs applied to his chest and abdomen for a quarter hour every other evening over a few months would have cost perhaps $25 for the cotton flannel and organic castor oil. A daily abdominal massage with castor oil would have supported weekly professional massage focusing on gentle clockwise belly movement and meticulous touch between the ribs, the intercostal spaces and at the sternum, the center of his body. This would have cost perhaps $40 to $80 per week.

The breathing exercises I would have recommended are simple: on an inhale raising his arms over his head, then bringing them back to his side on the exhale. In the beginning, expansion and contraction, motility, expiration and inhalation would have been almost nonexistent. But as he disciplined himself to repeat daily stretching, those cobwebs would have disintegrated and dissolved. Blood, lymph, digestive and other vital fluids and functions might have returned, gently softening his body. Gradually, his barrel chest could have adjusted downward by emotions releasing their grip on his thoracic diaphragm; his heart would have ridden lower, his kidneys would have drained more easily.

This treatment might have taken a couple of years to effect full healing, but the conventional treatment possibly offered him was almost certainly expensive and had evidently failed to help. I am sure pharmaceuticals were involved, but his structure—the connections inside the functioning body that housed him—were so compromised, drugs couldn't have done the job alone. This was a big strong man with powerful hands. Even in death his energetic body had presence. I am sure he would have had more to offer had he lived longer!

In this man's story, I see all of us. Lacking long run consciousness, we want quick fixes, so we pop a pill and hope it helps. High-tech medicine is vital when needed, and likely to be effective. But before heroic measures are called for, my preference is to work with interventions that both feel good and work effectively—interventions based on practical, time proven methods of care and healing.

It's easy to rush into the dazzling technologies and claims of allopathic medicine: we slip into thinking our illness "deserves" it. Often, collusion binds the patient and the disease. Your symptoms and treatments become your world, and you find it hard to see the bigger picture. As Dianne M. Connelly says in *All Sickness Is Homesickness*, "You have symptoms, the symptoms don't have you."[1]

My questions about the barrel-chested cadaver will never be answered. But for the rest of us, I have a plan. Balance the diaphragms: keep them toned, humming along in harmony with each other, with the sphincters and with the breath—three aspects of health, three vital "legs" to support you through the vicissitudes of life, no matter how old or young, rich or poor you may be.

Sphincters. Sphincters are ring-shaped muscles around the six external orifices of your body. They include: eyes and nostrils (each pair having two sphincter muscles but a pair counting as one for our purposes), mouth, belly button, anus, urethra, and genitals. (We also have internal sphincters easily abused by too much, too often or wrong choices in food and alcohol, but they are not my subject in this chapter.)

Healthy body sphincters relax and contract simultaneously.

As your diaphragms relax, coming to the natural dome shapes of rest, your sphincters relax. These actions of the diaphragms happen simultaneously with the functioning of the sphincter muscles. When we are healthy, there is a subtle rocking rhythmic beat, the balance of the dance.

What symptoms signal a sphincter out of control? Incontinence, flat feet, asthma, depression, hemorrhoids, smoking aftereffects, prolapsed uterus and varicose veins are some examples. All are treated by sucking water through a straw, vigorous closing and opening of the eyelids, and narrowing of the tongue! These simple exercises I do each morning while lying in bed are off-the-charts effective within days! For complete, easy-to-read directions I highly recommend *Secret of the Ring Muscles – Healing Yourself Through Sphincter Exercises* by Paula Garbourg.[2]

For now, let me share some of my favorite examples. Having delivered my whiz kid daughter in less than two hours, my pelvic diaphragm can always use a little attention. I also get wound up — "incorrigible" is a description friends use. These exercises help me unwind.

Paula Garbourg says, "Gently and delicately contract and relax the eyelids. This is a very good departure for normalizing the entire body. The motion is like the eyelid movement occurring during sleep." Do this for as long as possible without getting fatigued. She suggests fifteen minutes, but I never get there. Note: if you do this gently for thirty minutes or more, it will tune your whole system. What a warm-up for wannabe Olympian octogenarians!

Another eye movement I do for a tired back is vigorous closing and opening of the eyes. Shut your eyes tightly for several seconds. Then open them as wide as you can. Repeat. This is for overall body equilibrium. If I were president, these exercises would begin the Presidential Program for Physical Fitness.

A third eye exercise to synchronize sphincters starts by softening your jaw at the hinge, making space at the back of your throat. Keep your head immobile, using only your eyes, look as far as you can to one side and then to the other. It helps to pretend you will be able to see your ears.

Variations on all these exercises are found in yoga, tai chi, Aikido and a number of other traditions. Our cells know these self-care, self-balancing and restorative moves. Begin slowly and you'll be surprised at how much stronger you become. We want to be old ladies together, kicking up our heels when we want to and sitting in silence when we choose.

Organ Time. My tendency toward agitation sometimes affects my sleep, and as I love my sleep, this is a problem. My nervous system seems to have a mind of its own between one and three in the morning. In Traditional Oriental Medicine, this indicates that my liver is busy cleaning a very dirty house. Sleep disturbance is my number one "canary in the coal mine," my clue to whether I am taking some wrong steps. Depending on what time I awaken, I know a specific system is demanding attention.

According to Traditional Oriental Medicine, organs have a "high" time, a period in which they are "on." The qi flow begins in the lung channel and ends in the liver channel. The qi (or chi) flows like this: Lung, Large Intestine, Stomach, Spleen, Heart, Small Intestine, Urinary Bladder, Kidney, Pericardium, Triple Burner, Gallbladder, Liver. A lot of us experience wakefulness between one and three in the morning, liver time. Bless that liver, the organ of benevolence and human kindness, the organ of luster.

A few words about systems that span millenniums and cross cosmos: inspiring the innate body/mind/spirit healing cycles with movement—by needles, asanas, meditation or medicine—appears to be universal. Let us look at yoga and acupuncture and how each tradition might overlap.

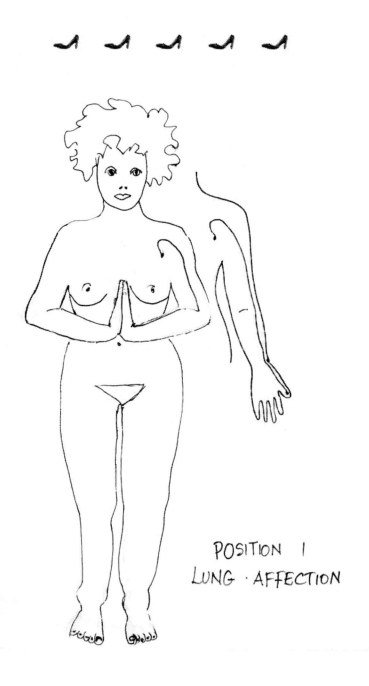

POSITION 1
LUNG · AFFECTION

Lung, 3 to 5 a.m. High time 4 a.m.: Appreciate every moment.
Recognize reverence in each breath. Pray.

Large Intestine, 5 to 7 a.m. High time 6 a.m.: Discriminates by reabsorbing useful fluids, eliminating unusable contents. Drink enough clean water. Support clean water for every being. Sweep and reach your arms to heaven. Change is the Law of the Universe.

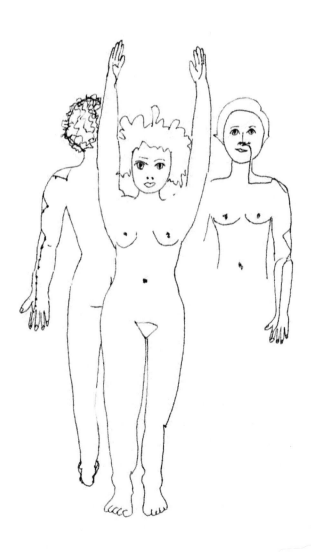

Stomach, 7 to 9 a.m. High time 8 a.m.: From the center of the body, the stomach–with the spleen–acts as one unit, transforming substances with alchemical wizardry: cantaloupe and cheese become breath and blood. Listen with your "gut." Bend forward, stomach resting on your thighs, induce activity. Utthanasana.

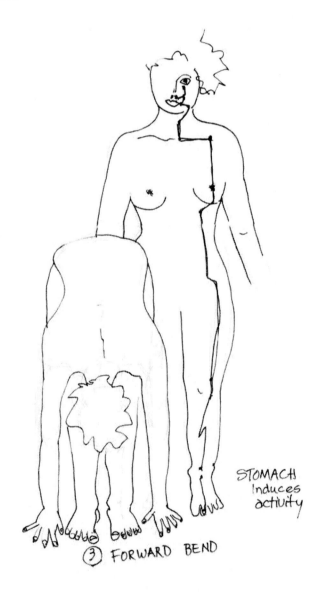

STOMACH
Induces
activity

③ FORWARD BEND

Spleen, 9 to 11 a.m. High time 10 a.m.: Faithful and reliable spleen (in partnership with the stomach) showers the world with creation: a song, a smile, a surprise. Stretch through your right thigh, calf and foot. Diffuse light. Lunge.

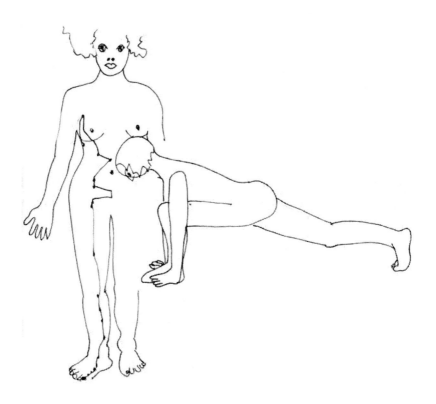

Heart, 11 a.m to 1 p.m. High time noon, just like the sun. Make time and space for energetic stillness.   Mindfulness comes from the center of the body. Use your joyous spiritual practice: yoga, tai chi, dance, prayers, art, martial arts, massage, meditation to support the Empress of Creativity: Communication/Interaction. (More about the heart and meditation in Chapter 5, Smiling.) Do a "push-up." Chaturanga. Make movement in the Heavens.

Small Intestine, 1 to 3 p.m. High time 2 p.m.: Discernment: sort out needed from not needed. Receive and thrive. Yes. Accept. Reject. No. Be clear. Dismiss "not yet, um, sort of, or maybe." Bow down. Prostrate yourself. Awkward caterpillar. Half chaturanga. All nourishing.

Bladder, 3 to 5 p.m.   High time 4 p.m.: The last phase of metabolic transformation, the bladder influences the vitality of the whole organism. Peace and satisfaction. Is this not the feeling that accompanies emptying your bladder? Lying on your stomach with your hands and arms in front of you under your shoulders, gently push your chest away from the floor. For this particular cobra, keep the back of your neck long, no wrinkles in the skin. Bhujangasana. Contains all wealth.

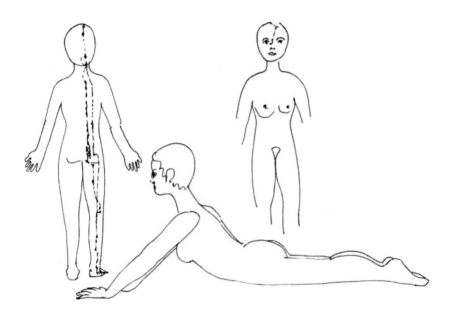

Kidney, 5 to 7 p.m. High time 6 p.m.: Creation of power manifested individually and evolutionarily as skill and ability linking the past with the future. From ocean depths to morning pee, our kidneys, another double organ (remember the lungs, eyes and ears?) filter and cleanse.

My personal qi opinion about the health of humanity: practicing more loving kindness might be the collective cure for backaches, the providence of distressed kidneys. Adho Mukhasvanasana Down Dog. Light possessing Rays. Put your kidneys in place.

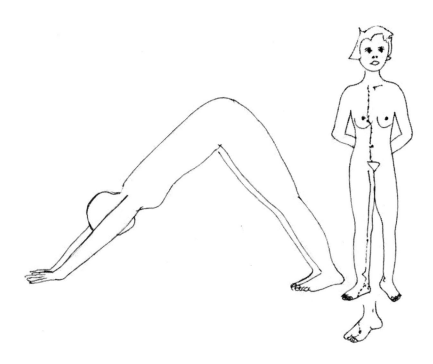

Pericardium, 7 to 9 p.m. High time 8 p.m.: This protective sac contains your heart and acts as a strong boundary against outside intruders. In Western medicine, the sac can shrink like cashmere or boiled wool, causing life-threatening heart muscle binding. Besides acupuncture and nutritional support for the heart, our antidote is generosity and conscious relaxation of jealousy and regret. Stretch through the left hip, thigh, calf and foot. Honor Aditi, Mother of God.

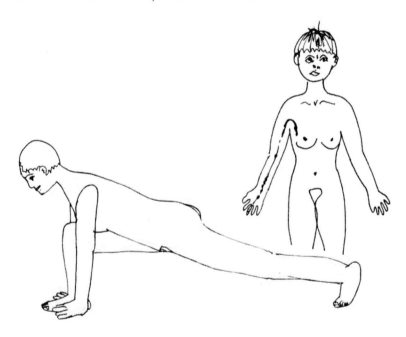

Triple Heater/Warmer/Burner, 9 to 11 p.m. High
time 10 p.m.: The triple heater/warmer/burner, orchestrator
of qi but not tied to a "body part" easily confounds Western
thinking. Yet even in Chinese medical writings clarity and a
conforming concept of triple warmer/heater/burner remain
inconsistent. Think of the triple heater/warmer/burner merid-
ian as regulating and maintaining body temperature by balancing physical heat, chemical reaction and pressure/rhythm.
Worship Life.
"I Love Lucy" or "The Daily Show With Jon Stewart" is often

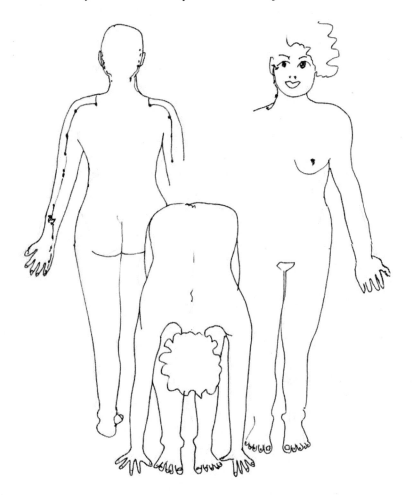

better for your triple warmer than the 10 o'clock news. Bend over and touch your toes. Or think about touching your toes. Stay there. Thinking, breathing, touching whatever comes within fingertips. My analogy of the triple warmer/heater/ burner is participatory democracy: education, commitment, compromise with respect for diversity allowing a powerful, unparalleled unity within the body.

Gallbladder, 11 p.m. to 1 a.m. High time 12 midnight : Partnered with the liver, the gallbladder is just and decisive. Gallbladder energy "begins." Even when influenced by physical or emotional shocks, the strong gallbladder decisively returns the being to one's unique life path. Antidote to being "galled" by politics or interpersonal treachery: share your gifts with others. Inhale. Stretch up. Reproduction of Everything. Go fat.

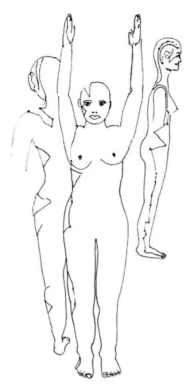

Liver, 1 to 3 a.m. High time 2 a.m.: The blessed liver, the visionary, modulator of engagement and self-restraint, speculating, evaluating, removing obstacles, allowing free circulation of qi; energy as blood, energy as emotions, energy appropriate to the circumstance. In my analogy, Jesus resides in the liver: benevolence and human kindness. Stand upright for kindness. Appreciate your good fortune. Luster. Tadasana.

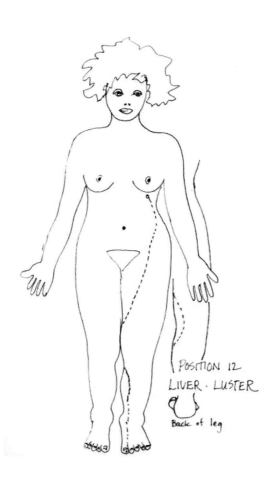

POSITION 12
LIVER · LUSTER

Back of leg

Sensory-Motor Learning. Another resource I recommend for anti-aging is a CD, "*Somatic Exercises: The Myth of Aging*," by Thomas Hanna, Ph.D.[3] It is a sensory-motor learning program for improving muscular control and sensory awareness. Exercises derived from Hanna's work and influenced by yoga are featured in Chapter 5, Smiling.

Thomas Hanna, a brilliant educator, believed in freedom, especially the freedom coming from unobstructed movement in our bodies. He, like other good doctors, believed that when we are supported for optimal functioning, we will nat-

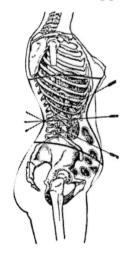

urally choose consciousness, which some call everlasting life. On this path, you are aware and observant, avoiding ruthlessness and recklessness. You opt for participatory democracy in your cells, your self and your community. Each cell is responsible and capable of healing. Like the diaphragms of your body, the springboard of youth, we need each others' voices and actions in our communities, sharing responsibility for a vibrant village and witnessing a sacred earth.

Tortured History. I look at my Jewish, Native American, Cambodian and Islamic friends and am thankful they are here, despite belonging to national, racial, political and ethnic groups targeted for genocide. My life is rich beyond measure because of their presence. Then, looking at history, I think, "Yee Gads! It is amazing any of us are here!" For example, gathering my resources for this chapter about the diaphragms of the body, I found in my paternal grandmother's college text, *Personal Hygiene and Physical Training for Women,* by Anna Galbraith, MD, another tale of torture and twisted ancestry.[4]

In a chapter entitled, "Dress: The Fundamental Cause of

Women's Physical Deterioration," the good doctor, thoughtfully and kindly teaching hygiene and training, takes on the history of the corset. Our genes are lucky to have made it through
the period the doctor describes, in which even tots were tightly
laced into constricting corsets. I include a section here to make
the point that it is not only the constrictions in our own bodies
by habits and emotions that interfere with the ability of our
diaphragms to function. Sometimes the restriction is cultural:

*The use of the whalebone corset prevailed even
among infants scarcely out of their swaddling
clothes. This was the natural consequence of the
pretended necessity to mold the human form in
order to obtain beautiful proportions, to reform
nature, and prevent her mistakes, and one could
never take too much care to obtain such laud-
able ends. Mothers who had neglected these first
indispensable cures for regulating body formation
would have been considered culpably indifferent
to their children*

*In women the movements of the upper part
of the chest are very conspicuous, the breast rising and falling with every breath. Whereas in
children and in men the movements are almost
wholly confined to the lower part of the chest, and
are called diaphragmatic, in contradistinction to
those seen in women, which are called thoracic.
It is now the opinion of many observers in this
country and in Europe that the habit of thoracic
breathing in women has been brought about by
constricting the waist and the lower ribs.*

*Observations made among Indian and Chinese
women show that abdominal breathing is natural breathing. Civilized women who wore no*

corsets had relatively good abdominal breathing. Further, a thoracic type of breathing can be pro- duced in men by putting them in corsets.

The greatest constriction produced by the corset occurs in the plane extending from the ninth to the twelfth ribs, which corresponds to the position of the diaphragm, stomach and liver.

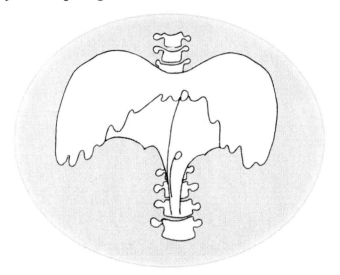

Dr. Galbraith quotes an 1889 paper that discusses the resulting damage to lungs and other organs:

Nature endeavors to make up this loss by the increased rapidity of the heart's action and more frequent respiration, but this is at the expense of greater wear and friction of the machinery. Pal- pitation and shortness of breath follow, and the woman is obliged to give up all active exercise.

Through this failure of the suction power of the heart there result disproportionately larger lower limbs and an accumulation of adipose tissue below the waist. This condition is much more common in women than in men, and is due to the lack of the heart's power to draw the blood back from the lower limbs against the force of gravity. Hence, the blood tends to linger in the lower extremities, interfering with the oxidation of the tissues.

The Relation of Corsets to Abdominal and Pelvic Disorders. *By constricting the lower part of the thorax, as we have seen, the action of the diaphragm is greatly impaired. This not only seriously interferes with its respiratory function, but with digestion as well, since by the active contraction of diaphragm inspiration, it presses down the liver and other abdominal contents, and produces a powerful massage of those organs, which aids in digesting food and in unloading the bowels; and, at the same time, the pelvis circulation is interfered with and pelvic congestion is favored.*

In case we are tempted to see history as a record of progress, it is interesting to read Dr. Galbraith's note that the barbaric practice of tight-lacing was introduced hundreds of years after classical Greek dress had established an androgynous and unrestricted norm:

From the time of Pericles, the great European distinction between male and female dress consisted in the length of the skirt—old men, priests, and officials being allowed the privilege of wearing long or women's skirts, and young girls being permitted to wear the short or "man" skirt. Among the Romans, this single garment, worn by both sexes, was called the toga.

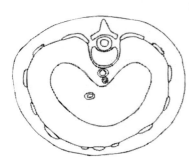

Corsets mutilated women's bodies from the thirteenth century to the 1950s. I remember my great-grandmother and my grandmother wearing cream, orange or pink-boned riggings. They were farm women putting on their best clothes, including a laced corset, for Sundays and dress-up gatherings.

This saga didn't end with my grandmother. I remember the "long-line" panty girdle I wore in high school, even as a cheerleader under Bermuda shorts. I still have grooves on my thighs where the "extra strength, double banded elasticized legs" (that is, tourniquets) cuts into my tissue. I wish I could say the long-line panty girdle was the last vestige of hobbling on the physical level in our culture. But in fact, having swallowed a steady diet of body constricting ideas of beauty when I was young—"there is a perfect girl-woman figure and it is not you"—I continue to hear it from beautiful young women today!

To what degree do we still accept restrictions on the movement and functioning of our amazing bodies in order to conform to an artificial standard? Are you lacing yourself into a corset, whether physical, emotional or spiritual? With help from each other, we can untie any corset.

Be My Valentine. You know the little "heart" sign that stands for love? Did you ever wonder how that symbol came to pass? I've looked at hearts. All kinds of hearts. Yet no heart—chicken, human, cow, elk or deer—has given me a clue to the abstraction that has became our symbol for the heart. Two side-by-side boxes with a couple of big tubes and four smaller tubes would better symbolize the heart. But as I was struggling to keep up with the medical students in embryology, I finally understood: ah-ha! The symbol comes from our bodies, from the part that holds our hearts, dancing to the beat of our lives. She's the thoracic diaphragm!

The heart rests on the thoracic diaphragm, which is where we find the perfect humps of the heart symbol. In fact, from the top down, the thoracic diaphragm looks like a heart symbol with a soft point. In a number of different body energy system theories, energy comes into our bodies from the back and leaves through the front. A good illustration is feeling the hairs on the back of your neck rise and taking action in response to that stimulus, being propelled from the back to the front.

The thoracic diaphragm, the muscle holding the bottom six ribs, hugs you around the middle. Your beating heart touches precisely on the central tendon. Anatomists refer to this central tendon as a "boomerang shape." Heart energy sent out does come back. The central tendon, white, because no blood is delivered directly to it, makes the spacious heart physically possible. In everybody, regardless of complexion, it is as white as an altar cloth, honoring the one heart we have in common. I like the way the Russian writer Aleksandr Solzhenitsyn speaks of it:

> *If only it were so simple. If only there were evil people somewhere else insidiously committing evil deeds and it were just necessary to separate them from the rest of us and destroy them. But the line dividing good and evil cuts through the heart of every human being. And who among us is willing to destroy a piece of their own heart?*[5]

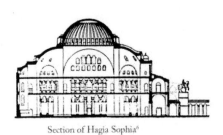

Section of Hagia Sophia[6]

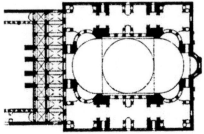

Section of Hagia Sophia[6]

The Resting Diaphragm Is a Natural Dome. I am sure the domed fashion of the Byzantine period (beginning around 500 AD) was strongly influenced by monks poking around in cadavers, naming body structures, identifying and admiring the thoracic diaphragm.

Besides holding us together, the thoracic diaphragm is a pump: she contracts and flattens out, making more space for the lungs to allow incoming air. Anchored at the bottom of the rib cage and pushing down, this muscle helps us poop, pee and deliver babies. The natural rhythm of inhalation and exhalation, like the waves of a calm morning ocean, changes space and pressure in our gut, stimulating the return of venous blood to the heart.

Treats For Your Diaphragms. One of the nicest treats we can give our thoracic diaphragm is stretching. Cats and dogs stretch, usually every time they get up, connecting their nervous systems to their muscular systems, leisurely elongating the spine, moving connective tissue that's inside the spinal cord. You do this too, whether you are a hotshot young pitcher or an ancient wise woman. Imitating the cat and dog stretch, waking up your spine, stimulates your diaphragm inch by inch, vertebra by vertebra, tuning your main trampoline.

Getting yourself into position should feel comforting, as if you could stay in this posture for five minutes, just breathing and quieting the mind. Master these simple forms of discipline not by pain toleration, but by strengthening the quiet mind.

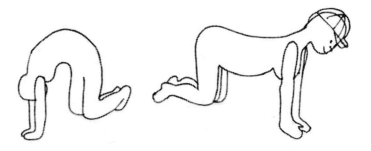

Start on all fours, arms straight with elbow crease facing forward. Hands under shoulders, fingers spread apart. Be meticulous with finger placement. Start with the little finger of the right hand placed directly under your right shoulder. Roll the palm of your right hand on the floor with as much spread in your finger webs as possible. If you are suffering from carpal tunnel syndrome, arthritis or any other hand trauma, protect your overused hands and wrists by modifying this position with raised support under the heel of the palm (such as a small pillow or rolled-up washcloth), fingers closer together, experimenting with comfort zones.

Observe placement of your knees. Are they directly under your hip joints? If this is uncomfortable on your knees, use padding underneath. Be neutral. Breathe. Your belly is lifting into your long spine. Use a mirror or a companion for feedback. Imitate a puppy. For a moment, wiggle your tail from side to side. Stop. Now drop your tailbone towards the floor, moving only your tailbone. You are not moving quickly, instead going slowly to be strong. Allow the next vertebra to follow, and the next, and the next, until your back is arched and your head is hanging. Breathe. Be a Halloween cat. Exhale. Inhale. Exhale. Do this gently, increasing the arch as you warm up.

When you are ready to switch, on the next inhale, move your tailbone skyward, toward the celestial energy field. Use only your tailbone as the prime mover. Breathe a complete inhale/exhale cycle. Gently lift the next vertebra from inside your lower front spine, as if your tailbone were a sacred snake licking the air for information from the stars. She is a shy snake, not pushing her spine forward but lifting from her long neck into her sleek belly. Just as the cobra has a fanning hood, your tailbone has her fanning hood, the pelvic diaphragm. Do not dump your belly onto the floor. Instead, controlling these stretching, lengthening, widening movements, use energy judiciously, observing with your breath each vertebra moving from inside your spine, your coccyx cobra tailbone lifting off the earth.

Continue this modified "dog" pose, making yourself into your own animal or vessel drinking in the heavens. Sometimes this spinal curve will be a sip; sometimes a long slow drink. But be careful and moderate: do not go to 100 percent of your stretch unless a qualified teacher is physically present. We all have overused and under used areas of our spines. When we are asked to stretch, our willing and joyous nature can take us to extremes, accidentally overextending already compromised vertebrae. If you go slowly you will involve the entire spine. Using your vertebrae equally, each according to its individual assignment, serves you best. From the cells of your spinal disks to the disk of the Milky Way, the universe breathes a sigh of relief.

The simplest breathing exercise for the diaphragms is to stand or sit upright with your arms at your side and your tailbone slightly tucked forward. Inhale with your mouth closed, the tip of your tongue resting upon the roof of your mouth behind your front teeth. If your neck and shoulders are not in pain, lift your arms up over your head. Hands directly over your shoulders, allow your fingertips to touch with palms facing each other. Exhale as you lower your arms. Pause for more than a moment. Start again. This time allow your arms to rise until you can feel your shoulder blades dropping. Raising your arms skyward is the task; the degree to which you touch the heavens is determined by your comfort, which may vary from day to day. You may be stronger and stiffer in the morning and more flexible and weaker at night. Morning arm lifting might stop below the horizon line. In the evening you may greet the high moon. Do five of these when you wake up and five before sleep, feeling the difference. Even if these are the only movements you practice every day for the rest of your life, you will be rich in blood and wealthy in mind, I promise.

If you are among the numbers of us who have stiff necks

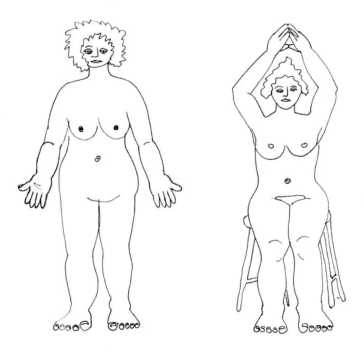

and shoulders, raise your arms in front of your body, not over your head. There should be no "crimping" at the tops of your shoulders. As you strengthen your trunk, you will be able to extend your arms higher over your shoulders. There is no rush. Move slowly. You are finding your wings. They might be deeply moored in a forgotten harbor. Shoulders are a mystery often taking years of respectful and grateful approach before they unleash their secrets.

Crossing the Midline. Physically crossing the midline of the body—right to left, left to right—also crosses from one side of your brain to the other and back. All body-mind disciplines cross the midline of your body, guaranteeing integration. Any activity crossing the midline of your body keeps circuits well tuned and energy juicy. Walking with arms swinging in rhythm to your footsteps, crawling, swimming, dancing, eye movement, yoga, Aikido and general stretching and twisting all increase vitality.

Breathing. When we inhale up, raising our hands, the thoracic diaphragm sinks: the dome shortens and flattens, pushing the soft stomach forward. When we exhale, the diaphragm returns to the top of her cathedral, pushing out the carbon dioxide and other wastes collected in the lungs. This liftoff creates rib action that is easily apparent, rolling outward and lifting up.

We support our dome by stretching and twisting, by bending forward and back, and by relaxing. Any movement involving the last six ribs directly contacts the thoracic diaphragm. Be careful with small repetitive motions in your life. Emotional restrictions occur on both sides of the diaphragm, limiting her mobility, preventing deep inhalation. When this happens, one quickly becomes short of breath.

"Breathe!" When commanded to breathe, what do you do? Inhale or exhale? Most of us think of breathing as sucking air into our lungs, using our nostrils as intake valves. But normally, no conscious act is needed: breathing happens by default in healthy bodies. You are breathing because the thoracic diaphragm is contracting, flattening out and changing the pressure in the chest cavity, which allows air to come into your lungs. Do not use your nostrils as suction pumps. Soften your belly, clearing space at the bottom of your lungs and at the tip of your tailbone.

You can hold your breath, but that only stops intake until your nervous brain stem overrides your thinking brain. In much the same way, you cannot stop your heart or slow your brain.

There are a lot of theories about breathing, some from ivory towers and some from the trenches. I am still observing. Observation has taught me some useful things.

Breathe through your nose. Your nose has a wonderful filtering system, a safety net that your mouth lacks. Your nose makes the temperature of outside air more compatible with your internal temperature before the air enters your lungs. Mouth breathing is hard on the tissues of your throat. In short, your mouth is for eating and your nose for breathing.

Listen to your breathing. A sigh of relief is a neurological utterance. A big exhalation often means sadness, as in a wistful sigh; an exaggerated inhalation often signals anger, as when nostrils flare. Held breath is a certain sign of fear.

I do know the ability to hold one's breath can be a tool or weapon. Choosing to hold my breath when sucked under water once made a nanosecond's difference from when my body said, "No more. You have to breathe." Inhaling in the white vortex of a 980-foot deep hole at mile 213 on the Colorado River, I stayed conscious. Churning, foaming white water had enough air in it to allow me breathing room. Sensory integration must have stretched my paddle, extended my body to catch the eddy, out of harm's way. If only the same sensory integration that kept me breathing at the Grand Canyon would kick in when emotional holes threaten to suck me under or intellectual corsets to bind me tight!

But if you consistently breathe shallowly or hold your breath out of anxiety, you are impairing brain and body functioning. Without sufficient oxygen, your thinking will be unclear and your digestion and elimination inefficient.

Breathing from exercise, breathing from vigorous exertion, breathing during sleep, rest and mediation and breathing colored by emotion are different but related animals, like monkey, gorilla, baboon and orangutan. There are a number of well-written books on breathing.[7] Attending to breath is essential.

Kissing Lessons. As I was sitting in silence on a ten-day meditation retreat, one of the first champions of this book passed on. Margaret was a woman who truly demonstrated loving her body. To her memory, I dedicate the story of kissing.

I met Margaret—tall, elegant and filled with humor—because I fell in love with her son. Smitten, I remained clear-eyed enough to know that if romance did not last with the son, friendship with the mother would. We made a pact. We were friends for life, confidantes, co-conspirators sharing astrological information and silly sexy jokes! She lived a fascinating and blessed life despite polio and several traumas to her back before she was twenty that left her coping with her share of misery.

She counted her blessings too: she had a fabulous husband, four spectacular children and a rich life in an intellectual community situated on a mountainside in southern California. Travel, good friendship, important and successful community work added to the stature of this impressive woman, who, as a child, thought herself too tall and too skinny.

After the passing of the love of her life, she moved north into a retirement home in our town. We spent at least an hour a week together. In the beginning, she drove to my office for appointments. As the years passed, I made home visits. Working on her feet, I heard the story of her courtships. Two different gentlemen approached. One, a successful businessman, asked after the health of her stock portfolio. The other, more curious about

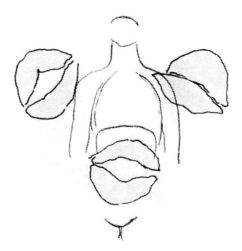

her life of travel, shared nature photo books while listening to her adventure stories. This second man, the younger, seemed the more promising suitor.

Margaret, even with back injuries, stood straight and tall. Her gentleman friend stooped, head moving forward. Wanting to make her prospective companion more comfortable, she took on the assignment of helping her friend feel better. Would I work on him too?

"Sure," I said, "I'll take his feet. You take his head."

On her next visit, Margaret told me that she had discussed kissing with this gentleman. He informed her that kissing was not his strong suit. They tried kissing. She reported that he was right: he needed training. He kissed with his lips drawn back, stretching them tight as boards, stiff and nonresponsive. I suggested his next treatment from me should be his head and neck. She was in charge of the rest of the training.

Some weeks later we had an appointment. The story of the romance was progressing, raising her children's eyebrows and generating sweet tales for the community. Everyone loves a romance, regardless of age. Indeed, when the couple is over seventy-five—when "We don't buy green bananas" is the standing joke—it seems especially sweet.

When she moved from southern California, Margaret let go of a huge quantity of material goods: a six-bedroom house filled to the brim with books, art, plants and furniture. Up north, her small apartment was filled with her favorite antiques, paintings and books. Only half joking, her family is convinced that in the case of an earthquake, photo albums and big books will bury her. While she was telling me the next installment of her romance, Margaret pulled off the shelf an oversized hardbound original edition of *Joy of Sex* by Alex Comfort.[8]

"Nathan rubs my back in the evening." This is good, I thought to myself. Margaret should have a back and foot massage every day. Most of us should have a back, neck and foot massage every day. "His kissing is improving."

"Bet his massages are more fun," I said.

"Yes, they are good. Makes me feel better." She handed me the book. "The other day after lunch, before my nap, I gave him this to look at."

Opening the maroon cover, I saw several yellowed Ann Landers and Abigail van Buren newspaper clippings with headings like "Sex for Seniors, Yes!" and "Kissing Is Good for Your Health."

"What happened"?

"He returned it before 5:30 dinner saying, 'Thank you very much. That was interesting, but I don't think I can get into those positions.'"

"Well, Margaret," I said, "with your kissing training and my foot work, who knows what miracles are in the heavens?" We never spoke of the romance again, but the next time I saw Nathan, he was brighter, taller, breathing easier in his chest.

Just kissing, the act of contracting one's lips, puckering up for a smooch, brings diaphragms and sphincter muscles into balance. Like all other exercises, it is better to do this at least five minutes daily. Do not fatigue yourself. If you are not currently kissing humans, animals, flowers and trees, try air kissing. The Europeans do it all the time, evidently knowing something we don't. Kiss yourself, arms and hands, and kiss the mirror. Your ring muscles and diaphragms deserve to be balanced and juicy, breathing in, breathing out, humming along. What better way to exercise than blowing a kiss?

❁ ❁ ❁

Notes

1 Dianne M. Connelly, *All Sickness Is Homesickness*. Columbia, MD: Traditional Acupuncture Institute, 1993. p. 63.

2 Paula Garbourg, *Secret of the Ring Muscles – Healing Yourself Through Sphincter Exercises*. Garden City Park, NY: Avery Publishing Group, 1997.

3 Thomas Hanna PhD (audio) "Somatic Exercises: The Myth of Aging," Novato, CA: Somatics Educational Resources, 1987.

4 Anna Galbraith, MD, *Personal Hygiene and Physical Training for Women*. Philadelphia, PA: W.B. Saunders Company, 1916.

5 Solzhenitsyn, Aleksandr I., *The Gulag Archipelago 1918—1956: an Experiment in Literary Investigation I—II.* New York: Harper & Row, 1973. p. 168.

6 H. W. Jansen, Ph.D, *History of Art.* New York: Harry N. Abrams, Inc., 1971. p. 171.

7 B.K.S. Iyengar, *Light on Pranayama. The Yogic Art of Breathing,* New York: Crossroad Publishing, 1972.

   Dennis Lewis, *The Tao of Natural Breathing: For Health, Well-Being and Inner Growth,* San Francisco, CA: Rodmell Press, 2006. www.dennislewis.org

8 Comfort, Alex. *Joy of Sex.* New York: Simon & Schuster, 1972.

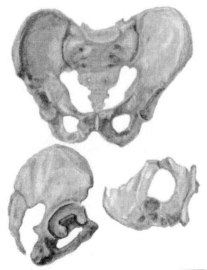

Marilyn Katzel

3

Buddha Full Belly

This chapter is dedicated to Yvonne Sligh, whose courage and creativity in confronting ovarian cancer is a story for the ages.

I gratefully acknowledge my yoga teacher, Mary Paffard and her colleagues and teachers, Barbara Benagh, Angela Farmer and Liz Koch.

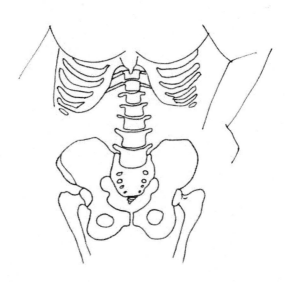

Witches Are Saints

How do we unlock you, Dear Belly?
Fiber by strand,
One by one,
Sharing silence with love, observation, breath.
Gut wrenching fear,
Exploding creativity
Dwell within your walls.
Deadly disease and joyful orgasmic celebration emanate
your cauldron.
How shall I worship you, Belly Goddess,
Keeper of the Universe?
I am you.
Match me.
Study my ways.
Follow my cycles.
Believe in me.
Cherish me.
Honor and respect me.

−DN, 1999

This is the belly chapter. Our dear bellies—the center of our middle age, big, round, laughing, breathing jelly—focus our cravings and aversions. Babies come from bellies. By water, fire, earth or air we return to the belly of the mother. My belly is a bowlful of beautiful, mysterious life and longing! Belly motion moves gazillions of dollars and millions of people everyday.

"Are you hungry?" my Chinese friends extend this traditional greeting.

"Starving for affection," I reply. "Hungry for love."

Who lives in the belly? What are its rules? Why do many of us want to lose our bellies? What does the belly teach us?

Years ago, someone studying body fat noted that you could pinch yourself around the belly. A pinch one inch wide was said to equal ten pounds of unneeded fat. I have always had something to pinch, less in summer, more in winter. Summer is the season of "natural weight"—the weight at which I feel most vibrant, energetic and comfortable—when swimming and hiking soothes bodies, fresh fruit and vegetables graces tables. Wintertime is the season of "stored weight"—the legacy of our past living off the land, making it through the cold season—as

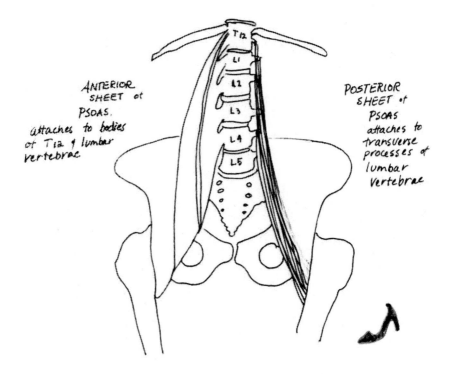

ANTERIOR
SHEET of
PSOAS.
attaches to bodies
of T12 & lumbar
vertebrae

POSTERIOR
SHEET of
PSOAS
attaches to
transverse
processes of
lumbar
vertebrae

we curl up to hibernate through long cold nights with popcorn and hot cocoa.

Most of my adult life I sought to control my weight, experimenting with the whatever diet happened to be popular. I could count on one hand the times I happily weighed in, satisfied with my size and shape: when I was pregnant, at meditation and yoga retreats when someone else cooks and in the warm summertime, when the fruit is ripe and swimming is easy. Now I realize the rhythms in my life will be both normal and natural. I prefer natural weight since it feels better. But a "storage" mechanism kicks in with cold weather.

Belly Belly Deep and Dark, What is Your Secret?

In the 1970s I studied with Al Graham, a renegade "rolfer," a model for Ida Rolf's system of structural integration, which at the time she taught only to medical doctors. Learning hands-on is my preferred method. The months of sequential deep connective tissue treatment I experienced unlocked my postural habits. Three times I repeated the entire series. Then I started training with Al Graham. Of my ten training sessions, the belly class was the most startling. On a "breathe into belly" command, starting on the right (liver side), he moved his straight fingers underneath my ribs into the center of my slow exhale. Another breath and he touched my thoracic diaphragm. Then tiny movements around the belly button, the umbilicus, moving in a circle; his fingers changed to a fist, continuing to move slowly right to left and top to bottom, like the hands of a very slow clock. My hard tummy softened with breath and pressure. With bent knees, feet flat on the table, heels lifting, heels dropping, toes lifting, toes dropping, he began again as my foot movements delineated the psoas muscle, the mother muscles of balance, deep diagonal branches from my groin pass my belly button. As he worked, the most extraordinary thing happened: my lower back heated up from the inside.

"Pilates," a movement discipline developed by Joseph Pilates, the powerful trainer of New York dancers, also focuses on the psoas muscle. In four-legged animals that wind up on the dinner table, we call this muscle the tenderloin. It brings us upright, lifting and rotating the thigh. This marvelous muscle weaves its way off the spinal trunk, branching like a Christmas tree. Often our backs hurt because some branch of the psoas is strained. The "top" psoas branch originates on both sides of the twelfth thoracic vertebra where our ribs end. With each lumbar (lower back) vertebra, another psoas branch adds to the body of the muscle until it crosses back to front, attaching inside the lower top of the femur or thigh.

Lie on your back, hands on your lower belly, knees bent and feet on the floor. With your fingers deep into your lower belly, slowly lift and lower your heels to feel the psoas' isolated work. She is a behind-the-scenes kind of muscle, but has so much power in the world, it will serve you to get well acquainted.

If you awaken with a tight lower back or go to sleep with a tired lower back, turn over on your tummy with a pillow or

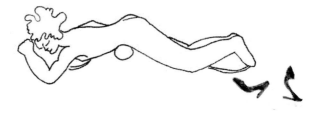

blanket roll tucked under your lower belly for five minutes. Anatomically, by placing a pillow rolled over the long way or a tightly rolled bath towel from one front hipbone to the other (across the anterior superior iliac spine, or "ASIS") you have placed the psoas muscle in a supported contraction. Turn your head in the most comfortable direction. After two minutes, move your head the other direction. I promise that a regular habit of treating your tired back with this support relaxes tight back muscles and methodically relieves many chronic back-aches.

Medically, I am not a fan of sleeping on your stomach, unless effectively propped to relieve weight off the soft organs. But with five minutes of the pillow or blanket roll shortening your lower back muscles, you and your nervous system will sigh a deep belly breath of thanks for the creature comfort inherent in release of strain or pain in the lower back.

Colon Camp. In the mid 1980s, two friends and I organized "colon camp," a ten-day retreat on a ranch in northern California. Patricia Howell made fabulous macrobiotic fare for meals and treats served between stretching, hikes, daily massage, swimming, quiet time and coastal adventures. When one of our guests returned to her hometown with a clear and happy colon, her local physician looked her over and declared, "You were on vacation. This won't last. You'll be back for meds!" He was right. When it comes to the health of the belly, diet, exercise, rest, meditation and sleep are all part of a regular program for healthy living. Our guest's fast-paced, irregular hours and highly demanding profession kept her body and belly on vigilant alert. Soon the effects of peace and calm, care and attention to her beautiful belly wore off. Her belly, inflamed, said, "I won't stomach this." The truth of the body is hard to hide.

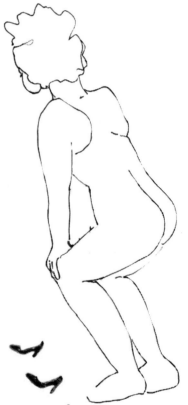

Awakening Belly exercises.
As Mary Paffard worked with teachers in other parts of the country, our hometown yoga classes felt their influence.

Lying on our mats, knees bent, feet on the floor, hands on our bellies, we spent hours observing our breath. We felt the exhale in our concave bellies and softening spines. We felt the inhale in our expanded bellies and the slight rocking of our tailbones—the "little bone of happiness," as the Cubans call the coccyx. When you inhale, the coccyx tilts away from the body; when you exhale, it moves into the body, a gentle wave lapping at life in the sacral cranial ocean.

Try some of the movements that worked for us: lying on your back, knees bent, feet on the floor, push your belly out, next dropping it into your spine, moving it to the right, to the left, isolating the movement of the psoas muscle, focusing on not using your always overworked back muscles.

Then, standing, feet hip-width apart, knees slightly bent, hands on your thighs, again push your belly out, pull it in to the right, to the back and to the left, waking up Buddha in the belly. As you play with these movements, be focused on your front belly motion. We tend to push from our spines and kidneys. Relax and drop your shoulders, slightly tuck your tail-bone.

Sound a complete exhale: moan, groan, oooh or aaahhh out loud as you release your breath. Breathing lightly, bring your belly to your spine, feeling it plastered against your back. Repeat, releasing and pulling back and forth, wringing out your organs, housekeeping your body.

Belly Balls and Belly Bolsters. The best little props to come from these teachers are belly balls and belly bolsters. In Chapter 1, The Sole of Being, I referred to foot or yoga balls, soft-textured rubber balls, often with soft spines or nubbles. What works for belly balls are usually available at your local pet or pool store. Years ago, before this exercise equipment was available, we used "dead" tennis balls on pressure points. Tennis balls are still useful, especially for neck support instead of four-inch diameter pool balls which lift the neck too high. The secret to making tennis balls work is to put each in a stray sock so they stay put when propped against the neck.

You make your belly bolster yourself: it takes only five minutes and might save your life. Take a large bath towel or lap blanket you can set aside as a body prop. This prop could be the same roll you designed for your lower back. Check to be sure the material is long enough to cover the distance from your pubic bone to six inches above your head. Roll the towel up precisely and tightly. Bind it with a cord or rubber bands in the middle and at both ends, securing a long firm roll. Turn three inches of one end of the belly bolster back over itself. Secure it with a strong rubber band, old necktie or stray sock to create a bulb at the end of the long tube. Things seem to get stuck in the belly, such as indulgences in the culinary department, emotions, bad posture and physical indiscretions. The belly bulb helps to release them.

Belly Bolster Exercises. When starting the passive exercise I am about to describe, you might like your belly bulb to be smaller. I tend to vary the size, particularly when traveling or after sitting for a long time. DO NOT DO THIS EXERCISE IF YOU ARE PREGNANT OR ON YOUR PERIOD, OR UNDER A DOCTOR'S CARE FOR DISEASES OF THE ABDOMEN.

On your hands and knees, place the bulb end of the belly bolster under your body. The long tail of the bolster parallels your spine. Slowly lower yourself onto the bolster, the bulb above the pubic bone, midline, below the navel. Gently impale your lower abdomen on this bulb, lowering all of yourself, midline, onto the length of the tube, turning your head to the left or to the right, whichever side is more comfortable. The sensations are sometimes a bit strong for a few moments because the true belly, soft, pliable and strong, is usually tucked away behind a barrier of unneeded tension, old habits and bad attitudes. It can take a little while to find that soft pliable belly. If the belly bolster feels extremely powerful, rest on your elbows and forearms so there is less of your body weight on the bulb.

As the middle belly relaxes, roll a little to the left, then a little to the right. Move slowly, exploring uncharted territory. When you are comfortable with the belly bolster in the center of your body, roll slightly so that the belly bolster is on your right side for a few minutes, with your left side dropping toward the floor. Then reverse to the left side. Be sure to go to the right first: in more than 99 percent of the population, the right side of the belly is home to the iliocecal valve, the doorway from the small nutrition-absorbing intestine (the ileum) to the large fiber-and-toxin-flushing intestine (the cecum). Often, when you experience back and head aches, the iliocecal valve's door is fluttering, letting toxins back into the small intestine. The belly bolster is a wonderful tool for at-home treatment to remind the door of the iliocecal valve how to close.

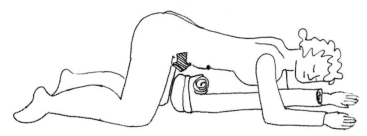

After you have rested for a time with your head turned one way, turn your head to the other side. If your neck is stiff on the second side, prop a small pillow or folded towel under your shoulder on the stiff side until your neck relaxes. With time and practice, the second side will turn as easily as the first. If both sides are stiff, use props under both shoulders.

Remember the belly bolster is not medical treatment for serious illness but a tool for personal, individual self-care. Yet the belly bolster has been known to identify silent killers in the abdomen before other symptoms appear. If you experience unusual symptoms such as bleeding outside of your normal cycle, see your doctor. If something unusual does appear, real attention by a competent health care provider makes the belly bolster worth its weight in gold.

Ball Exercises. Lie on your back, knees bent. Place a ball on either side of your spine at the bottom tip of the scapula (your shoulder blade), usually at thoracic vertebra eight. These are the bony bumps your fingertips might touch when you give yourself a bear hug. Get close to the tip of the shoulder blade without being right on it. Sometimes the muscles feel better having the balls hug the spine and other times your back will want the balls farther out toward the shoulder blade. Rest there, observing your breath. Your muscles will start to soften. Lightly rolling, move a little from side to side. Move a little from head to tail, gently rocking. After a few minutes, move the balls to the sacrum, the broad V-shaped bone above your tailbone. Keep your knees bent. Rest there, observing your breath moving into your lower belly. With the balls still at the sacrum, bring your knees into your chest. This should feel very comfortable. It is not a stretch or a crunch. There are no prizes for getting the knees on the chest. We do this to soften and round the supported back. Let your knees move from your chest toward your axilla (armpits). After a few minutes, release your feet to the floor.

Another good place to use the balls in a passive practice is at the widest part of the calves. As I wrote in Chapter 1, The Sole of Being, the backs of the calves have an intimate relationship to the mind, and both work overtime. So try it again: lie on your back, putting the balls under the calves. Hang out, listening to your breath. Releasing the calves helps to release your most stubborn thoughts and feelings.

Now nestle the balls next to the cervical spine, your neck. This takes a bit of doing. You may need a little towel or sock placed laterally outside of your neck and the balls, to get completely comfortable. Be sure your chin is not higher than your nose. Support the back of your head with a towel so there is no strain or jamming in the back 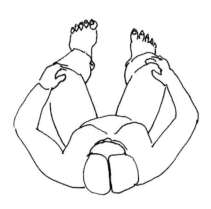 of the neck. Feel the back of your neck and shoulders with your fingers. Baby-soft is the quality you are seeking. Breathe, and let your muscles soften. Touch your neck as if your fingers were those of Aphrodite, the Goddess of Love. They are.

Do not push your kidneys forward. Find your kidneys by putting both of your hands over your lower back ribs. Thumbs toward the outside, fingers pointing toward your spine. As you inhale and exhale, feel your breath moving your hands and kidneys in and out, expanding the sides like bellows.

Most of us push from a few places with unfortunate results: our necks, our voices, our kidneys. An extreme view of kidneys pushed forward looks like an ad for push-up bras: lifted breasts in front crunch the kidneys in back. Similarly, too-high heels put the kidneys in a vice grip. Pushing kidneys forward often results in cold feet and bad circulation. When you push your head forward, out in front of your heart, you court respiratory difficulties, heart disease, upper backaches and migraines. Bodies out of alignment look uncomfortable and age faster. At any age, evenly used bodies are prettier and happier.

In yoga, the corpse pose is exactly what it sounds like: flat on

your back, letting the floor do all the work. Let the balls rest in
the natural curve of your hand while in the corpse pose, with
your feet eight to twelve inches apart. Check that your forehead
is level with your chin.

Around the same time we were belly breathing in yoga class,
several accomplished body workers shared with me similar
weight loss and belly health secrets from Asia. "Love your belly"
consciousness is all over the world. Victoria Jett, a practitioner
in San Francisco, recommended deep belly self-massage. With
a closed hand, massage around the pie of the belly slowly, vig-
orously, even jump from one side to another arousing the juices
and saying hello to the bowl of life. Move your hand clockwise
if constipated, counterclockwise if afflicted with diarrhea.

In the winter of 2001, I attended a Stanford University
School of Medicine symposium on lymphedema. It was ser-
endipitous. My dear friend Alan Carpenter had been to Grand
Rounds at Stanford Hospital the previous day. He was taken
with a presentation by Dr. Stanley Rockson, who had devoted

his life to that neglected stepchild of modern medicine, the
lymphatic system. In all of my medical anatomy books, there
is not one detailed drawing or rendition of the complete lymphatic system, only shorthand representations of the system. A
drawing that accurately depicts the lymph system in our hands

and feet would leave room for nothing else: no blood, no bone, no muscle, just lymph channels.

The lymphatic system was discovered in 1622 by the flamboyant Italian anatomist Gasparro Aselli. One day, he was dissecting the abdomen of a dog. With great theatrical presence the surgeon opened the peritoneum (sack of the abdomen). As he unfolded the colon, exposing arteries and veins running through the omentum—the sheath holding all components of our guts—Gasparro Aselli was stunned. Startling everyone in attendance, a third line, yellow-white, appeared alongside the arteries and veins. What could this third circulation system be? It took the flamboyant physician a few days to figure out 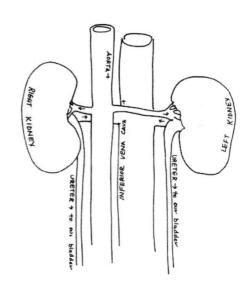 the dog had eaten a meal shortly before its death. The newly observed system carried the fat away from the stomach.

Lymphatic vessels around the stomach transport fat. What a clue, women! The fat we eat—good, bad, supportive or destructive—starts it journey from the stomach through the abdomenal lymph system. In middle age especially, the lymph system needs support for us to be healthy. Several practices can help. Dry brush massage is one: use a natural bristle brush to brush the skin, just as you would brush your hair, to stimulate your circulation (brushing toward the heart helps). Lymph needs to circulate, but the system doesn't have a pump other than your own exercise. So massage and oiling with edible oils and lotions stimulate the flow of the lymphatic system. Resting your legs up a wall and wearing compression garments help too, as observed in Chapter 1, The Sole of Being.

We're not talking about huge effort here, but tiny steps, one step at a time, will add up over the years, so that when I am an old lady, my shoulders will support my weight going upside down because my lively belly and balanced psoas muscle will lift my legs over my body!

The community in which I live has wonderful live theater, the Ukiah Players.[1] Every year, local people create and perform monologues about their own lives. The stories are presented to the community under the title "Telling the Truth in a Small Town." The following is a monologue created and performed by Yvonne Sligh, to whom this chapter is dedicated:

> I was dying. I guess I really knew it—I had a feeling that something was terribly wrong with me—but I told myself it was my imagination.
>
> My story begins with a false sense of security. In 1993 my doctor said I needed a hysterectomy. "While we are at it," he said, 'let's take everything out—ovaries too. You're old and you don't need those organs anymore.'" I was in my forties at the time and didn't feel old, but when he said that a big benefit to doing the total operation was crossing ovarian cancer off my list of things to worry about, I decided to follow his advice. Since my mother and father had both died of cancer I had developed a phobia about that dreaded disease.
>
> In the summer of 1995, I began to have abdominal pains. I went back to my doctor and he ran tests, but not for ovarian cancer. That had

already been ruled out because of the hysterectomy. The tests came back showing nothing. During the next seven months I went through periods of pain and distress, and from one doctor to another. Each reassured me that nothing was wrong. One man even gave me a prescription for tranquilizers and told me I was creating my own misery in my mind. As I sat there talking with him that day, I had a belly full of tumor and a lung filling with fluid. If only he had taken the time to pick up his stethoscope and put it to my chest—

Right after New Years, in January 1996, I collapsed with a pleural effusion—my lung filled with fluid—and was hospitalized. A young Asian-American doctor took my case and, ruling nothing out, discovered that I had ovarian cancer, stage four—the most advanced and worst possible diagnosis. What lay ahead for me was surgery—five major surgeries that year—and chemotherapy. I was well for awhile, but then it came back in the summer of 1998, and I am battling once more.

I am going through chemotherapy again, taking taxol—the drug that comes from the yew tree—and cisplatin. It has some very unpleasant side effects, like complete hair loss, nerve damage, and other things I won't go into. I am also trying alternative therapies to keep myself in balance, like meditation and tai chi and massage therapy. I quilt. With each stitch I take, I pray. I've heard of recent medical studies showing that sick people actually get better after writing about old traumas and hurts. Now I have a lengthy journal in which I write every day. I'll try anything.

My message out of all of this? Women who have had their ovaries removed can still develop ovarian cancer. There can be tiny amounts of tissue left behind and a few cells are all it takes. I have heard people say, many times, that this cancer can be prevented by a hysterectomy. Not true. Please tell all the women you know. Finally—listen to and believe your own body. If you know something is wrong—it is. Never let anyone tell you that you don't know how you really feel.[2]

I want to underscore Yvonne's poignant rule: *"Never let anyone tell you that you don't know how you really feel."* Now let me offer several more rules for the belly. If you are "going on a diet," the first rule is do no harm. In the words of the Hippocratic Oath: "Primum no nocere." The kidneys, honored to be the only organ in our bodies to which blood is supplied at a 90-degree angle, are terribly vulnerable to crash diets. Kidneys sit on either side of the spine, precious organs doubly protected by renal fat and a bag inside more fat and another bag. This is the human equivalent of the brown animal fat called suet, stirred into Christmas puddings, or used to give extra support for birds in extremely cold weather. When we go on starvation diets for a couple of days to lose four or five pounds, the numbers may change on the scale but some of the first weight to melt away is in those protective bags of fat around the kidneys.

"Fat is fat," you may say.

Not exactly. In chapter 4, Eating, you will learn how good fats and bad fats are different. Our Creator packed the kidneys into a double bag of fat to keep them in place, at a right angle to the blood supply. When we chase after rapid weight-loss, losing our kidneys' packing material, these organs drop, putting a crimp in the hose that channels our blood supply. Headaches, sore backs, sluggish elimination, fatigue, poor posture, general depression and all sorts of old-age markers appear as a result. Dropped kidneys can stay that way for years. Treatments include standing on your head, hanging by your knees on the monkey bars and more belly massage. The massage to "lift" the kidneys goes like this: lying on your back, knees bent, put straight fingers into your belly, below your navel, as deep as you can go and lift toward your head. The motion is in and up as if you are lifting those little babies back into their sacred cradles, or do a down dog yoga pose.

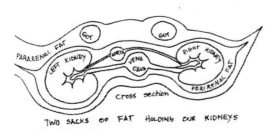

Cross section

TWO SACKS OF FAT HOLDING OUR KIDNEYS

This is one of the first remedies I try when I get a headache. Headaches are usually messengers. Someone needs to be attended to now: colon, sinuses, kidneys, muscles, eyes, blood sugar. One headache carries twenty or thirty possible messages. How to heal the head? Start with the obvious: enough rest, more exercise (less if you're overdoing it). The number one cause of headaches in the United States is muscular tension.

Let's say you arrive at my office with a headache. I immediately start by working on the neck and head for ten minutes. As quickly as possible, I move to your feet, since they tell me so much. Your feet will tell me if your colon is sluggish, the second most common reason for headaches: too much is being asked of your digestive tract, too little is being asked of your muscles.

What we ask and how we ask our digestive tract to perform directly links to our emotions, because our Buddha full bellies think. We have an enteric brain!

An Enteric Brain? Entrails as in intestines and guts for brains? Yes. We have an ancient brain humming along independently of the brain in our skull. Or we could think that our gut brain, the enteric nervous system (ENS), is an older evolutionary sibling to the cranial nervous system (CNS) which we consider to be The Brain. The ENS and CNS are made from the same parental material, the fetal neural crest. With communication hardwired between the gut and the skull brain, the upstairs and the main floor brain share a plethora of chemicals, commanding instructions and mechanical informants. In fact, for every command coming from the upstairs brain, CNS, to the ENS, the main floor brain, there are nine commands sent from the gut, ENS, to the upstairs brain. A lot of the information from the gut to the upstairs brain is "field" information, informing Headquarters of gifts and grudges that have entered the gastrointestinal system through the mouth.

Why is this not common knowledge? Actually, in the language of our culture it is common knowledge: *gut instinct, funny feeling, foreknowledge, queasy, visceral response, intuitive* remind you of a few of our references to knowledge flowing from the center of our bodies.

This is another curious story of competition and rivalry among the medical profession which held information hostage for almost fifty years. A British physiologist, John Newton Langley (1852–1925), in 1921 published *The Autonomic Nervous System* in which he advanced the concept of an autonomic nervous system including sympathetic nervous system (Yikes! Run for your life!), parasympathetic nervous system (Ah, nothing better to do than take a nap in the hammock) and enteric nervous system (How shall we digest this acid tomato? alkaline chard? slightly rancid food? Self-clean? Collaborate with the immune system to defend the bowel? Absorb and propel nutrition through the digestive track?).[3]

As owner and editor of the *Journal of Physiology*, Langley

demanded strict adherence to style and often rewrote academic papers to meet his journal requirements. At the time this must have been quite controversial as well as professionally irritating to the authors because upon his death, the concept of enteric nervous system was reclassified by members of the Physiological Society as parasympathetic relay ganglia, part of the vagus nerve/vagal supply that directs gut motility. Seems like a meager comeuppance to a dead Langley but an abrupt halt to cutting-edge intuition accurately describing human physiology of the gut.

In any case, investigators focused on new research in chemical neurotransmission: acetylcholine and epinephrine (later to be corrected to norepinephrine). In 1967, Michael Gershon, MD, proposed a third neurotransmitter, serotonin, which cracked open the reality of the enteric nervous system. Ninety-five percent of all serotonin is produced in the gut. Now it is generally recognized that "at least 30 chemicals of different classes transmit instructions in the brain, and that all of these classes are also represented in the ENS."[4]

The story of the gut measuring up to "brainy architecture" is logical. Worms, our ancient evolutionary ancestors, and our twenty-first-century newborn humans perform the same two actions immediately and well: eat and digest. Then both beings rest and restore. Brain one: survive. Evolution, in the brilliant

reality of waste not want not, kept the first brain. Why discard a good thing? Leave the gut brain, the main floor brain and move on to the protected vault, and the central nervous system.

Highlights of Contemporary ENS Research. Investigations of the enteric nervous system might forecast disease: foreign bodies, plaque and neurofibrillary tangles identified with Parkinson's disease and Alzheimer's disease have been found in the bowels of patients. A simple rectal biopsy might conclusively identify these diseases at an early onset instead of waiting for an autopsy.

We know that mood-altering drugs used to treat emotional illness in the upstairs brain affect the main floor, gut brain, often causing diarrhea and constipation.

Conversely, when a very small dose of conventional pharmacological antidepressant therapy is given to people with functional bowel disease, symptoms are often relieved! ENS responds dramatically to changes in serotonin levels.

Most of us are on emotional diets. We have ideas about what we will and won't eat that can actually endanger our health. A while ago, I took a call from a man traveling the world. He contacts me every few years when some health situation causes him concern. He was calling to ask for help for his new girlfriend, who suffers with genital herpes. She had tried her arsenal of vitamins and minerals to no avail. I believe a herpes outbreak indicates depletion. There are various fast-acting remedies, which is what my friend wanted for his partner's pain. One remedy might be dependent on blood type: her blood type was O. My suggestion was to consume fatty acids in the correct proportions: four omega-3s to one omega-6, including conjugated linoleic acid (CLA), an antitumoral, and protein, all in food form, the body's favorite way to ingest solutions.

Even though they live in an area where grass-fed beef is available, she was not willing to eat the food that might be the best medicine for her condition. Meat was not acceptable, because she was a committed vegetarian. Meat had not passed her lips for twenty years. Maybe she suffered through a longer recovery by maintaining her path.

In the mirror image of this situation, a lovely obese woman I know is addicted to milk. She drinks a gallon a day. Milk makes her happy, so giving up milk to stay off blood pressure medications by lowering her weight is not acceptable. So now she's experiencing the side effects of blood pressure medication.

Cravings and aversions have more control in our lives than we recognize. "Do no harm" is a hard one when the enemy has outposts in our heads, our taste buds and our emotions. What are your cravings and aversions? What ideas claim territory in your well-being and Buddha Full Belly?

Tummy Tender,
Secret Witch,
Housing sick,
Shield the innocent,
Feed me your wisdom.
Vibrate life.
Hold tradition.
Cradle my soul.
Rock my movements.
Laughing from lips
South of the Bible Belt,
Sing me your secrets!
Ageless Divine Tummy,
Witness these vows.
Tucked away savings.
Hope for me yet.
You are mine. I am yours.
Identify my foolishness.
Never lose me,
Tender Tummy.

—DN
July 25, 2001

❀ ❀ ❀

Notes

1 Ukiah Players Theatre, 1041 Low Gap Rd., Ukiah CA 95482. www.ukiahplayerstheatre.org

2 CA-125 controversy. CA-125 test is not 100% accurate and is, therefore, not considered by most physicians to be a good screening for ovarian cancer. Approximately 80% of women who have ovarian cancer will have an elevated CA-125. Approximately 20% of women who have ovarian cancer do not ever have an elevated CA-125. That is why it is critical to use the CA-125 only as part of a diagnostic regimen that includes a rectovaginal pelvic exam and transvaginal sonography. www.ovarian.org

3 John Newton Langley, *The Autonomic Nervous System*. Cambridge, England: Heffer & Sons, 1921.

4 Michael Gershon, MD, *The Second Brain*, New York:Harper Collins, 1998.

4
Eating

Eating well is not rocket science. I grew up a tomboy, preferring manure and horses to baking and braising. But anyone can function in the world of pots and pans. I get by with simple and nutritious foods. No matter how busy or confused, you too can take tiny steps in the direction of green and good. Your body will thank you.

What you eat is directly related to how you feel, think and age. There are a few foods that are highly beneficial for everyone. Besides water, the first lady of life, we all need protein, carbohydrates and fats. But in what forms? Generally, the more processed a food is, the less value the food has for your body. Some bodies need cooked food, other bodies need raw food. Some bodies need to eat meat, other bodies do well leaning toward vegetarian fare. There are healthy foods some people should avoid because of individual sensitivities: one woman's food is another woman's poison. Food is fuel, food is drug and food is medicine. Know your food friends and food enemies: whatever agrees with your digestion, is easily assimilated, lets you sleep through the night, doesn't constipate or cause you flatulence is a friend.

As a child, I imagined the hunter-gatherers from whence we all descended finding food and gobbling it up the way I sometimes inhale food in my consumer-consciousness trance. When

I eat with friends, I usually slow down. But still, I am often the first one finished.

Two hundred years ago local indigenous nations chose from over four hundred different kinds of food. By our contemporary standards, if you consume fifty different kinds of food you are an adventuresome eater! Diversity of diet and slowness of consumption: two important aspects of healing eating.

The knowledge and information I have are gifts from eternity. They are not secrets. They are in you, too. You have to listen for them. In every little way our bodies work or fail to work, there are truths to be learned. In every bite you put into your mouth or every drop of oil or cream you dab onto your skin, there are truths to be learned. When asked if I am "New Age," I laugh, because much that I know is as old as the body. My standing joke is, "I am ageless."

How to Eat. For years I experimented with diets, eating, food and nutrition. Not even fashion has so many fads as diet. And clearly, one diet doesn't fit all. Some people do well with a basic meat diet, and others cannot handle the high protein. Inuits don't do well on papaya and pineapple. They need the high fat not the high sugars. So when you try any food or diet, pay attention to what your body tells you about how it is meeting your needs. Are you sleepy after eating? Do your poops move easily and completely? Are you maintaining a glowing luster in your eyes, skin and hair?

It's not just *what* you eat, but *how* you eat, *when* you eat and *where* your food comes from. If a high-protein diet is for you, it is even better if the steak is from an animal you hunt yourself or purchase from a local farmer/rancher, grass-finished animals being the best. Grass-finished animals supply us with conjugated linoleic acid (CLA), an antitumoral, and omega-3 fatty acids. They are also lower in cholesterol than meat from animals fed on grain, even if the grain is organically grown.[1]

How much you eat is important. Health spas have a reputation for giving teeny tiny portions while buffets are famous for challenging you to eat all you can. My opinion echoes Weight Watchers' point system, which assigns zero points to many vegetables. The bells and whistles of satisfied sensation and natural weight are to eat for the best taste, then stop. Your body provides a reality check. Hungry, starving and being truly empty are not the same. In this country, very few of us ever get empty, yet a lot of us are close to nutritional bankruptcy. Our dietary needs change by age, exercise, repair, seasons and, if we are willing, sense.

Science doesn't always equal sense. Scientists in 1900 believed that babies needed calories in ratio to weight. If a 150-pound man needed 2000 calories a day, a ten-pound baby needed only one-fifteenth of that: 133 calories a day. Good thing no one could talk the babies into being satisfied with 133 calories a day! That is beyond starvation. In truth, babies need 2000 calories a day, as much as it takes to maintain a grown man, because they are fueling rapid growth.

Open your hands and make a bowl. What you can hold in your cupped hands is the amount of food you should put in your stomach at any one time. When you fill yourself beyond that measure, leaving no air space, your stomach has no room to mix juices. It is as if you have a tiny mixing bowl and too many ingredients. They spill over in the form of diarrhea, constipation or gas trying to move forward or they spill backward in the form of belching, cramping, acid reflux, disturbed sleep and nightmares. When they spill, overindulgences become harmful, jumping into other systems. Americans spend gazillions of dollars each year on digestive aids. Quantity control saves your skin, your sleep and your senses! Eating the right amount is an internal insurance policy.

When you eat is also important. I walk and eat at the same time, a habit that would send my great-grandmother into a spin. She was a tiny woman who lived in a big house purposely built with counters and sinks fitting her stature. When I visited, my young body also fit. I call on body memories to help me remember her way of living. Each night, dressed in her gown and robe, with a long braid trailing down her back, she prayed on her knees next to her bed. She was meticulous about sitting down to eat breakfast, lunch and dinner at the same time each day. She drank green tea for breakfast. She ate slowly. Often, she had two or three different simple vegetable dishes: cooked carrots, string beans and boiled new potatoes. They came from her garden, even in the winter, when home-canned veggies were taken down from the larder or long-stored raw ones were dug out from under straw blankets covering the garden beds.

As I write this description, I hear my daughter's voice: "Yeah, yeah, and you walked barefoot through twenty feet of snow, sixteen miles to school every day." But in truth, my great grand-mother's sensibilities are more like what I wish for my own life than my current habit of tossing almonds into my mouth as I hurry down the hall returning phone calls between clients. In fact, I have noticed that if I sit down to eat my food—snack, breakfast or dinner—I maintain my weight. When I start eat-ing as I am moving—in the kitchen, out the door, on the road—pounds sneak around my middle.

Eating late at night is hard on older systems. For those of us over fifty-five, eating the last meal of the day by 5 P.M. gives melatonin, the sleep stimulator, time to saturate our tired, wired brains. Most of us do best by breaking our night's fast the same time every day, around 8 a.m., which is stomach time in the system of Traditional Oriental Medicine. I wake up early and have hot water and herbs for my first drink. Unless my appetite is depressed because I am sick, by 8:20 my stomach and head complain if I am tardy with the protein.

When food is prepared with love, you can taste it. In season, organic, fresh and least-processed is best choice because you don't want to consume pesticides and other pernicious chemicals along with your dinner. Use the precautionary principle: besides the traditional risk assessment, answer these questions: Is this food safe? Are the chemicals in this food necessary? Err on the side of risk avoidance.

Eat for Your Heart. Put your hands together in prayer, palm to palm. Bless your life and your body. Fold your fingers so the hands still mirror each other but now look like two fists. This is approximately the size of your heart. This deep, dark, red muscle always moves, over one hundred thousand daily movements. How faithful! How committed! The heart is a true servant, but if you make it a slave to your wildness and indiscretions, the servant will rule the master. We now know from science what we have naturally known for centuries: what we eat changes the course of disease, particularly heart disease.

Let us chew on the practice of eating. Chewing is a miraculous practice, addressing problems from indigestion, insomnia, aging and constipation to weight gain. Add juicy saliva enzymes to the act of chewing and we initiate digestion in the mouth. Chewing promotes patience, conservation, beautiful skin, knowledge and…floating poop. (By old naturopathic standards, floating poops were one of the most important signs of a healthy lifestyle, indicating the correct ratio of carbohydrates, fats and proteins in one's daily diet. How wonderful to have a built-in mechanism, a Geiger counter for nutrition!)

Sitting, focusing, eating slowly seem to be components of a healthy lifestyle. When you chew, you also initiate and stimulate the flow of digestive juices farther down the alimentary canal. Remember the enteric brain? Chewing thoroughly not

only improves digestion but also acts as the doorbell announc-
ing guests. Swallowing large chunks of food quickly puts more
pressure on your stomach, as if the guests barged in before you
were dressed for company. Your cranial brain is also stimulated
and soothed by the action on your teeth when you chew, another reason to happily chew and take care of your teeth.

Go slowly to move easily. Of course, with all the other miracles of life simmering along in our bodies, this too is common
sense. The gift of life is a miracle—in mathematical terms, a
rarity—that should be honored. Step by step, cell by cell and
stroke by stroke, you swam from the cosmic ocean into this life.
Now you are awake enough to choose consciousness! All your
steps in life deserve your attention and focus, without haste.

A Few Simple Eating Guidelines. Don't mistake thirst
for hunger. Do not eat when the saliva does not flow. If you
think that you are hungry and you are not salivating (juicing up
in your mouth), you are thirsty. Drink clean, noncontaminated
water instead of eating.

Lists. Writing down what I eat changes my intake. Often we
have completely skewed ideas of ourselves and our behaviors,
for example, how much and what we eat. The most powerful
behavior change you can do today, without costing you a cent
or compromising your senses, is keeping a precise list of what
you eat. Note quantities as carefully as you note dollars and
cents in your check register. If you have pancakes for breakfast,
specify "two pancakes, four tablespoons of maple syrup and one
tablespoon of butter." Noting what we consume ignites a light
of awareness that, with intention, can be translated into behavior change—if change is needed.

Throw out the corn syrup. It is a fake and a wannabe, one
of the chief poisons we consume, often daily. Even processed
sugar is better for your pancreas than corn syrup. Food manu-
facturers use corn syrup because it is cheaper, but it is one of

the major culprits in our epidemic of diabetes, because it is such a fast, hot fuel (similar to alcohol) that it distorts our digestive process, like throwing gasoline on a fire that should be burning slowly and evenly. Read the tiny type of the back of the label (they don't have to tell the truth on the front) and avoid anything that contains the words "high-fructose corn syrup," or just "corn syrup." Keep current reading the labels. These guys are slick.

Avoid iced beverages. Almost all healers from all traditions counsel avoiding too-cold drinks. Icy liquid arrests the digestive process, leading to many problems. Eventually, the chain reaction slows the elimination of toxins, causing swelling in the joints. If you enjoy cold drinks and experience stiffness in your hands or feet, try an experiment: drink room temperature or warm water or other beverages instead of iced drinks for two weeks. The same goes for ice cream and other extremely cold foods.

Acid-Alkaline Balance. Years ago, naturopathic teaching counseled eliminating refined sugars from our diet, since they produce acid fluids in our bodies. Too much acid causes what used to be called "acidosis," leading to premature aging, dyspepsia-agitated digestion, general fatigue and all around ill health. The naturopathic approach was to cleanse your system with local fresh vegetables cooked into a broth systematically eliminating all refined foods. This information has now entered mainstream medical journals. There is a relationship between eating sugar and joint pain. For most of us, alkaline foods put our bodies into fabulous balance. Here's a recipe for that vegetable broth, to restore balance:

You'll need a pressure cooker or steamer, filtered water and approximately three pounds of fresh in-season green vegetables. Use at least three varieties, such as kale, zucchini, cabbage, celery, onion, green beans and spinach. Soak your vegetables in cool water for ten minutes. Cut up and cook under pressure for ten minutes with two cups of water or steam till very tender. When cool, add fresh herbs to taste and whir in the blender until pureed. Add water if necessary to produce a total yield of six cups. Refrigerate in a glass container. Drink one eight ounce glass twice a day, one in lieu of dinner and the other as a pick-me-up during the day. Try seasoning with a dash of good balsamic vinegar or Bragg's Liquid Aminos, available at the health food store. Be sure that your other meals are made from foods that are local, organic and satisfying. You are on the alkaline trail of beautiful skin and healthy insides.

Eat Your Beans. Several years ago, I was given a beautiful pressure cooker. Do you remember pressure cooker horror stories your mother or grandmother used to tell? If not accorded due respect, I was told, pressure cookers became bombs, blowing roofs off houses, sending shrapnel in every direction. I easily absorbed kitchen wisdom about taking caution with fire and knives. But while I comprehended the danger of blowups, I never understood how to keep the tool from becoming a weapon.

I wasn't the only one. To cook beans or seal canning lids, avoiding food poisonings like botulism, we were told the "bobber" which lets out pressure had to whistle a particular note. It was not easy to distinguish the tone of happiness and health from that of death and destruction. I suppose that's why my mother and almost all of her friends kept their pressure cookers in the basement. If they were ever hauled upstairs, the bobber top, technically called a regulator valve, was seldom to be found. "Rummage around in the top drawer," I was told (the top drawer resembled Fibber McGee's closet, so it took quite a bit of rummaging). "See if you can find the bobber top for the pressure cooker." Health and happiness prevailed: the only time we found the bobber top was when we cleaned the drawer, never when Mother cooked.

My plan for my new high-tech, state-of-the-art European pressure cooker was to increase my intake of beans. Canned beans make up the bulk of my emergency supplies for earthquakes, millennium madness and other natural and unnatural disasters. This is how often I went for beans: once a millennium. I decided if I was to write about food, I surely needed to include the marvelous attributes of beans and therefore I needed to do research into beans, from plant to poop, which meant eating a lot more.

Beans in every stage of life pack power punches. As a plant, beans bless the soil with rehabilitating nitrogen and other essential nutrients. Bean fiber cleans the colon like no other broom; well-cooked beans equal colon health. The unused sugars and protein, unless thoughtfully treated, pack a intestinal wallop. And as nature always has the last laugh, beans are the one food guaranteeing floating poop.

Following the directions as to timing and ingredients, rinsing them well and sorting through them for pebbles, I made pot after pot of beans. I especially liked kidney and white Great Northern beans.

Are all beans created equal? Ninety-five percent of all soybeans and soy products are genetically modified. I do not eat much soy. When I do, I prefer genetic antiques without modification. Old beans take longer to cook than this year's crop, but appropriately stored beans retain their nutritional value for years. Soaking eight hours makes a huge difference in the amount of time it takes to cook beans. Cooking in a pressure cooker reduces cooking time by hours. In the time they take to cook, the amount of fuel used and the proportion of vitamins and minerals remaining in cooked beans, pressure-cooked beans win hands down.

Kitchen folklore is full of legends about how to reduce the gassiness of beans. Some say that completely cooking the bean protein eliminates the fuel that converts to methane gas in our colons. Besides shortening the cooking time, a good long soaking, changing the water regularly, is said to make bean protein more digestible. Cooking them with onion and carrot is also supposed to absorb the gases. I happily compost the cooked onion and carrots just in case. I've also experimented by pouring off the cooking water halfway through the cooking process, replacing it with boiling spring water to keep up the temperature. See what works for your digestion: this is one place I believe our collective research will pay.

Observing your ancestral history, what did your great-grandparents grow? How does your diet differ from theirs? We, as Americans, blessed with fabulous diversity, often get sidetracked by nutritional fads and glossy ad campaigns.

Experiment by eating beans grown in your biological ancestral farming history. Make note of the cooking process and keep track of methane produced in your body after you eat them. Personally, I find varieties of beans that are easily grown in Iowa, Sweden, England, Germany, France and Scotland—places in my own gene pool—easier to digest than exotic beans. But it could be my imagination.

The ultimate solution is "Bean-o," the health food product responsible for eliminating gas in my most adamant bean-eating friends. One drop is all it takes to convert the methane power of beans.

Some Truths About Fat. The most recent great wave of popular mistranslation of scientific factoids concerned fat. We were told to cut fat, but as it turns out, food without fat isn't as tasty. Thus, products with reduced fat have added sugar to compensate. Every year this country produces twice the calories needed for every man, woman and child. Competition to sell food products is fierce. Seduced by low-fat promises, consumers are subjected to increased sugars, the bane of our pancreas! Each bite we take of unneeded, overprocessed carbohydrates takes a bite out of our pancreatic tissue. As a result of the no-fat fad, America now has an increase in diseases of the pancreas, including diabetes. Advertising and pseudoscientific half-truth, bad research and economic greed have produced a great and unforeseen ripple effect. As new research now hints (and old common sense dictates): better to eat fat consciously and in moderation.

I am crazy for oil, like the rest of the world. I love to taste it, eat it, smell it and smear it on food and skin. I am very picky about the quality of oil I taste, eat, smell and smear, and so should you be, at risk of your health. Oils make our cell walls. When we misuse oils and heat, we make impermeable cells which hold toxins the way a hungry dog holds a juicy bone.

Not all fats are suited to all uses. My recommendations about safe use of oils are based on the research of Mary Enig, PhD.[2]

Some natural fats and oils should not be heated: flaxseed oil, unprocessed cold-pressed canola oil, unprocessed cold-pressed soybean oil and any other highly polyunsaturated oil. Heat deforms these oils, making them rancid: bad-tasting and poisonous.

Natural fats and oils appropriate for cooking, salad dressing, and one-time frying (that is, where the oil is not reused) include corn oil, peanut oil and olive oil. However, allergic reactions and aflatoxin contamination (a form of mold that contaminates peanuts) are reasons for not using corn or peanut oil. Pay attention to how your body responds when you eat corn or peanut oil. Even if you are not allergic, you may discover a sensitivity that makes it best to avoid them.

Natural fats and oils safe for deep fat frying include coconut butter and oil, butter and ghee (clarified butter), palm oil, lard, tallow, high oleic safflower oil, high oleic sunflower seed oil and regular sunflower oil with added sesame oil and rice bran oil.

Contrary to misinformation released by the hydrogenated oil

industry, coconut oil is a healthy naturally saturated vegetable product. Unhydrogenated coconut oil contains fifty percent lauric acid, "good fat." Unhydrogenated coconut oil is made of

After Queen Lewis Chessmen 12th Century

mostly medium-chain fatty acids. Our bodies metabolize unhydrogenated coconut oil efficiently and convert it into energy. We do not store unhydrogenated coconut oil as fat. It does not elevate "bad" cholesterol (LDL) levels. I use Omega Nutrition brand, which is unhydrogenated, containing no solvents, protected from light damage, and with no trans-fatty acids to ingest.[3] Look for these identifying characteristics in your coconut oil products.

Another eating layer, another story about my dear grandfather. When I asked my mother if someone we knew was a farmer like Grandpa, she said, "Oh, no. They are dry land farmers. They grow crops. Your grandfather has animals to take care of too."

Indeed he did: herds of cattle, flocks of geese, chickens, guinea hens, horses, ponies, an occasional mule, schools of fish as well as groves of conifers, grassland pastures, lakeside cottages and more. As the eldest grandchild, it was my special blessing to visit the farm for several weeks each summer. I spent one summer devising schemes that would allow me to live with my grandparents all year. Life in town with my siblings and parents was fine but I loved life on the farm. I wanted to be there the whole year round to see the comings and goings of the animal and plant life and observe farming through all four seasons.

One particular summer I remember clearly. I experienced first hand what he called "a wild goose chase."

At the end of the day, Grandpa, showered and dressed in soft, old, clean clothes, reclined as far back as the big La-Z-Boy chair would go. Next to him on a TV tray was a cup of black coffee cooling in a saucer. This was most often a quiet time, as he reported on the events of the day: "Who had the Black Angus bull for breeding next month?" or "Tomorrow, I'm heading south to Plover to pick up the Holstein."

I knew the language, the images that went with the names: short, stocky Black Angus and big, black and white Holsteins or medium sized red-bodied, white-faced Heifers. Grandpa knew their personalities. Grandma listened as she moved about the kitchen in a neat dress, apron and sensible heels, frying and boiling food to within an inch of recognition.

Sometimes his day featured a particularly unsuccessful row with animals or humans which ultimately accomplished nothing except a dramatic and exciting story before supper.

In years gone by, Grandpa had stallions he lent to other farmers for breeding their mares. Then tractors came on the scene and farmers no longer needed workhorses to pull plows. He let go of the horses, keeping just a few for us to ride. My horse, Star, was a central player in my life even though I only got to touch, ride, smell and play with her a couple of weeks out of each year. Star and I had primary roles in one of the biggest wild goose chases ever, when we took it on the chin. Actually, we took it on the shoulders.

The herd of bulls needed to be moved from the north eighty acres to the farmyard. The "north 80" was a little over a mile from the farmhouse. In Iowa, gravel and dirt roads divide almost every square mile of land into a neat grid. You can travel across the state in any direction the wind blows without ever needing a highway. Even today this transportation network makes riding horses and bicycles a dream come true.

When there was a roundup, everyone on the farm helped except Grandma. On this occasion, I was thrilled to be part of the team which included three horses and riders. My uncle was the leader, so dashing on his quarter horse, Spook, a paint.

The young hired man was on the Shetland, Lightening. I was bareback on Star, a sweet Morgan, just a hand taller than the Shetland but tall enough to present a challenge. Unless someone gave me a hand up, getting onto Star required standing on a tree stump, water tank or firm fence.

Grandpa asserted that you were not a horsewoman if you needed a saddle. The only way to ride a horse was like the Indians, bareback. I might saddle up once or twice during my visit, depending on how much time the adults had to help me or check my technique with the girth, the belt under the belly which held the saddle in place. But for the most part, all riding required was a cob of corn to catch the horses and a bridle.

Heading for the north 80, Grandpa drove the big truck. Along with two more men in the truck and the two men on the other horses, we headed north.

To my nine year-old eyes, the north 80 was a gentle rolling hill. The cattle stood at the bottom of the hill, on this side of the creek. That was good. It meant we didn't have to deal with a steep bank or water crossing. Moving them would be easy. Riding behind the herd, shouting "Yeah-ha, giddy-up!" was as much an excuse for my lungs to express happiness as to alert the cattle that we were there.

Halfway up the hill, a bull cut out of the heard. Grandpa shouted to me, "Darca, you get 'em."

Star and I moved out, cutting him off, preventing him from heading down the hill. The Black Angus paused, turned, gazed at us. He looked at the herd moving up the hill then turned back towards us and charged. He hit Star's shoulder, throwing me into the air. I landed on the bull's backside and rolled off. Star rolled too, then got up. The bull charged, rolling my pony a second time. I scrambled to my feet and headed up the hill. Star too got to her feet and headed up the hill. The bull ran down to the creek.

Shaken but whole, both Star and I were glad to be back on

top of the hill. Petting her, cooing, stroking her shoulder, I found no cuts. I touched her a lot the next couple of days. She was one stiff horse.

Grandpa told Grandma the story while she fixed supper. "All those men," he exclaimed, "and not a thing we could do about it." Thank God I was riding bareback! Bound to a western saddle, he said, I would have likely rolled with my pony and "creamed my young innards."

Queen of
The Rancho

This was not that bull's first transgression. Out on loan to a farmer, he had gone after another animal. The bull became hamburger. We ate a lot of hamburger that winter. We ate local.

Remember the Precautionary Principle: err on the side of risk avoidance. Ask these questions: Is this safe? Is this legal? Are these additives (chemicals) necessary? Wherever possible choose organic cold-pressed oils. Avoid oils if their labels say "genetically modified," because "genetically modified" safety has not been proven. Ask for butter and ghee to come from grass-fed animals. If you can choose, for the reasons described earlier, grass-fed is best. Read the contents of everything you eat. When "hydrogenated" or "partially hydrogenated oil" appears in microscopic type, put it back on the shelf.

By returning to the shelf crackers, cookies, salad dressing, ice cream, candy and potato chips made with the "bad oils," we are saying "No!" to breast and ovarian cancer, liver toxicity and hormonal distress. One warrior at a time, we make an army, returning the unacceptable to a food industry that should not be allowed to choose cheap over healthy. This may not stop the epidemics immediately, but it may improve our odds of being healthy. This doesn't mean we have to give up our treats. They are on the supermarket shelf in the form of Häagen-Dazs Vanilla and Coffee ice creams, of Trader Joe's Yukon Gold potato chips made with olive oil. By searching, I eat less of the hazardous oils. You will too. But don't assume your favorite ice cream is still using whole foods. Regularly check ingredients.

Feeding Your Skin. Be equally cautious with body lotions and skin oils. Almost everyone I touch in the course of my work is too dry: your skin needs to be fed. Your skin eats everything you put on it, so here's a rule: do not put anything on your body you would not put in your mouth. Imagine a plate of pasta covered in a popular yellow creamy skin lotion. Yummy? Mineral oil, a primary ingredient in these concoctions, is completely indigestible. It's made from petroleum by-products and carries away your fat-soluble minerals. Dead swamp material was not so good to eat a million years ago, before it became petroleum. Why would it be good aged?

Read the contents of any lotions you consider buying. Better yet, make your own skin lotions from your kitchen supply of cold-pressed organic, exotic oils. My favorite concoction—sweet, easy and the basic recipe for all my skin formulas—contains ghee (clarified butter) coconut oil, cocoa butter and shea butter from Fair Trade Africa, India and Central and South America. Ask your local health food store or your market's organic department to special order these products for you if they are not already on the shelf or in the cooler.

Here's my treatment formula: Use eight ounces of ghee, fourteen ounces of coconut oil, as much cocoa butter (pure and preferably from a candy maker) as needed to add a deliciously sweet chocolate aroma and as much shea butter as you can afford. Shea butter is expensive and worth every penny because it goes on your delicate skin! It's the most emollient oil in the world; it comes from a tree in Africa. Keep track of your recipe, since you will happen onto your own best ratio, judged by aroma, skin texture and other subjective criteria.

If preparing the above formula is more than you want to do, buy three separate edible oils to mix for your skin. Choose sesame seed oil, cold-pressed coconut oil/butter, and castor oil from the health food store. Do not buy the toasted sesame oil suitable for cooking Chinese style unless you want smell like a kitchen. In a ratio of 1:1:1, heat on the stove until well mixed. Cool. Rebottle into the original glass containers or store in glass mason jars. Label. This is your basic nutritional skin formula.

A bath is the best environment to pamper your skin, unless you have a water filter on your shower head to remove the chlorine. Remember from chapter 1, The Sole of Being, that we all do much better in nonchlorinated water, which is less drying to skin and hair. Turn back to that chapter and follow the instructions for dechlorinating the bath water. As I fill the tub, I allow the hot water to run over my tightly closed container of base nutritional formula or edible oils, warming the contents, thereby making the oil treatment more therapeutic.

Now massage and oil your body with the warmed oil. Be sure to include all sides of your ears and nostrils and navel. Be meticulous. Get into as many cracks and crevasses as you are willing to touch. Let the warm oil soak in for a few minutes. The drier your skin is, the longer you should wait to get into the tub. If necessary, reapply oil until your skin has a generous coat of nutritional oil. Warm water opens the pores of your skin, allowing the oil to saturate deep into that dehydrated hide. There are few areas of your body that need gentle soap: face, underarms and the dark, moist external genitals. No need to use soap anywhere else! Dry off. If you do not feel a light coating of oil on your skin, once again massage warmed oil into your skin.

Wait a little while before you dress, or wear something you have dedicated to oil treatment. Often women complain about getting their sheets oily with this type of nighttime treatment. I figure you have one body to care for and a multitude of sources for sheets. I recommend you identify those clothes and sheets you are willing to sacrifice to the greater good of your cells. When I go to a meditation retreat, I pack a wardrobe dedicated for wearing after oiling, assuring me that oiling before and after every shower will not be a concern. These are comfort clothes, serving me well for sitting and for soaking up the healing power of fat.

AFTER FRIDA KAHLO

Try applying the mixture of oils or a single oil to your hair one day a month or once a quarter. Leave the oil on your hair for 24 hours. Before you are ready to wash out the oil, make a container of equal parts shampoo and spring water. Most shampoos are too strong for our hair. I prefer not to use shampoo containing sodium lauryl sulfate (SLS).

In my experience, oiling serves us in at least four ways. First, it lubricates: skin sucks up warmed cold-pressed organic oil like a sponge. Second, it nourishes: oil goes directly into the skin supporting the lymphatic system, carrying vitamins and minerals. Third, oil preserves: we age because we dry out, so oil keeps us young. Finally, oil protects: from personal experience, I am convinced that oiling your skin provides extra layers of energetic protection. When dirty deeds are coming down the pike, if I am oiling regularly, I feel that cushion of time and comfort help to keep me centered. This is similar to the way I have heard antidepressants described: three feet of space between agitation and myself, a layer of protection holding me gently in the universe.

Ghee whiz. Fat is good. The right amount of fat keeps us lustrous; the right kind of fat keeps us alive. Being partial to butter, I like ghee. Ghee is one of the best oils to use for cooking because you can heat it so hot and not have its molecules flip tails to form impermeable cell walls. I recommend *Ayurveda: The Science of Self-Healing* by Vasant Lad for information on this fabulous fat.[4]

Ghee is a mainstay of Indian cooking and a great skin emollient. Here's how to make your own: put one pound of raw, unsalted organic butter over a medium flame until the white saturated fats condense and fall to the bottom of the pan. Heat until the ghee starts to boil and froth rises to the surface. Skim off the foam. Turn the fire to low. Your creation will start to smell like popcorn and match the smell by turning a golden yellow. Taste it if you want—I like the taste. To tell when the preparation is cooked, drop a couple of drops of water into the pot. She'll crackle when she is ready. This takes a while, so be patient.

Turn off the flame, let the ghee cool until it has hardened. At the side of the pan, use a teaspoon to lift up the edge of the hardened ghee which makes a hole in the surface: pour off the milky watery dregs. Toss the dregs into the compost. Heat the ghee again and pour through a cheesecloth-lined strainer into a clean container. This will remove any remaining residue from the precious oil.

On my trip to the moon, I will take ghee. Ghee removes clogs throughout the body. During hay fever season or when I must stay in forced-air-heated homes or ride in airplanes, I put a dab of ghee on the tip of my little finger (nail clipped short) and massage the inside of my nostrils to protect my tender tissues. You do not have to refrigerate ghee, but you must store it in a cool, dark place.

Years ago I started dating the lids on my jars of stored ghee. An old Ayurvedic practitioner once told me that 100-year-old ghee would cure anything. Some people age wine, I age ghee. These days we can buy organic ghee directly from the health food store or online. Yearly, I put away a stash of unopened ghee for prosperity.

Almost the last word on ghee from Ayurveda: avoid ingesting equal amounts of ghee and honey at the same time. They have equal but opposite therapeutic powers, pulling the body in opposing directions: energy and movement with honey and substance and solidity with ghee. Usually, people who are wiry and nervous should have more ghee and less honey; those who are lethargic and stolid should do the opposite. I make a concoction of one-half cup ghee and one cup of honey to spread on my toast. This seems to give me even energy without exciting my pancreas and adrenals.

If you need to gain weight, bless you: make a pot of one-half cup of honey and one cup ghee. Use this consistently to gain the kind of weight you need to protect your bones and add substance. Note that aged organic raw honey is also a medicine.

Cod Liver and Castor Oil. Are you old enough to remember swallowing cod liver oil—the antique form of vitamin A—during the cold and flu season? My tablespoon of oil was usually followed by a slice of orange, rendering both orange and oil into yuck in my visceral memory. Better to get your oils today from eating healthy fish and save your taste buds.

If ghee is the queen of oils, castor oil is the chicken soup. On several occasions use of castor oil packs saved me drastic medical interventions. Remember in the introduction I mentioned knee surgery? Well, years after surgery, I was kicked in the right thigh by a stallion, reinjuring the repaired knee. I went flying through the air and landed in a heap in the corner of the corral. I managed to limp up the hill to the ranch house. By the time I got there, I couldn't move my leg: as I look at my leg now, I can still see the horse's hoof imprint. I lay down, elevated my leg and applied castor oil packs—a dozen layers of cotton or wool flannel saturated in warm castor oil and applied to the unbroken skin. I applied the pack for fifteen minutes every hour while I tried other remedies (such as the homeopathic remedy arnica for mechanical stiffness and crutches). Within ten days I could walk without pain, and I escaped the surgeon's knife entirely!

Taken internally, castor oil is used for constipation. Castor oil comes from the castor bean, *Ricinus communis*, which grows on the castor tree in the tropics, castor plant farther north. It originated in Africa or India. Egyptian tombs sealed in 4000 BCE contained the seeds of the castor tree. The oil may have been used for lamps as it was some centuries later, but knowing a bit about those fabulous oilers, the Egyptians, I like to think they expressed the nontoxic oil for beauty and medicine. In the 1800s in Europe and the United States, this gentle purgative became the medicine of choice in treating constipation due to inflammation of the abdominal organs.

A Castor Oil Story. Mr. Farmer, a ninety-four-year old retired professional living in Philadelphia, came to see me because his grandson gave him the gift of a foot massage. Listening to his story was a delight. During his long professional life, after completing his daily responsibilities, he used his evenings to paint oil portraits in his studio. On weekends, his pleasure was ballroom dancing with his wife. Every quarter, without fail, he invested in the stock market. This was a wise, wealthy and happy man.

Now his feet hurt. His family had no money for shoes when he was growing up, so, like the Chinese upper-class girls who had their toes wrapped under their bound feet, his toes crowded on top of each other and curled around because he wore too-small hand-me-down shoes. As he aged, the malformed toes hobbled and limited his range of motion and balance.

While I worked with his feet, Mr. Farmer's sounds of joy and sighs of relief filled the treatment room. "It feels so good! Where have you been all my life? Will this make me younger?" Toes started to uncurl; muscles awakened; movement, color and warmth washed through his whole body. He was in good shape. He just needed some regular work with castor oil, the lubricant of choice for adhesions (stuck spots anywhere on the body). As we worked, I reminded him that sipping water throughout the day would help his body flush the crackles and crunches from his feet.

"Your feet will change," I said. Self-massage, sharing foot massage with his dance partner or going to a regular massage therapist would change his feet over time much more than we had managed to change his feet in the hour we worked together.

"Oh, this feels so good, so alive! I feel twenty years younger!" As he exclaimed, he wriggled his whole body. Then, as if the thought had just struck him, Mr. Farmer said, "But if my feet change, I will have to get new shoes!"

"New shoes would be good," I said, "especially shoes made for your feet."

"Oh, I can't get new shoes, that would cost too much."

"Well, see how you feel today. Then decide about shoes."

He never bought new shoes, but he did come back for more treatments. Now I have a lovely nude painted by Mr. Farmer hanging near my front door, reminding me that bodies easily change with time and sometimes ideas in our minds are set in concrete.

Eating as Spiritual Practice. All spiritual and health practices teach us how to eat. For example, the Northwest Coast Native Americans worshipped Salmon God, organizing their community and life around the life of the salmon. When the salmon were ready to spawn, the priests and doctors prayed day and night for direction until they had received in dreams detailed instructions from Salmon God. Men walked out onto the sandspit, poking holes into the sand to allow sea and river water to wash away the sand gate. This sacred communication allowed the salmon to swim upstream at their most fertile time.

Food is a universal metaphor for all forms of sustenance, which is why so many teaching stories turn on food. Consider this one: identical banquets were spread out in Heaven and in Hell: mounds of fresh ripe fruit, aromatic and juicy; platters of steamed, raw and baked vegetables, prepared with exquisite spices and flavors from every cuisine. Think of it. Exhale, then take a breath imagining all your favorite foods and drinks laid before the folks in Heaven and in Hell.

The Heavenly banquet is filled with laughing, happy people, dining, singing, conversing, enjoying delicious food and drink. But in Hell, seated around exactly the same table, the people are sad, frustrated, angry and starving! Guests at both banquets are equipped with yard-long utensils. In Heaven, each diner uses the yard-long spoons and forks to feed the person across the table. In Hell, the frustrated diners try to feed themselves, but their arms are too short to convey the tender morsel into their own mouths.

A clever man in Hell gripped the neck of the spoon close to its bowl. Pushing a scoop of yummy mashed potatoes into his mouth, he whacked two other people with the long arm of his uncontrolled spoon. Offended, they struck back. Before long, everyone was throwing punches, dashing the platters and morsels of fabulous food onto the floor! As always, greed creates anger and frustration. Except when traveling by airplane (when you are reminded to put on your own oxygen mask first), offering food to others first serves all of us best.

❉ ❉ ❉

Notes

1 Jo Robinson, *Pasture Perfect.* Vashon Is., WA: Vashon Island Press, 2004 (previously published as *Why Grass Fed Is Best*).

Grass Finished Beef available from Robert (Mac) Magruder. magruderranch@pacific.net

2 Mary Enig, PhD, *Know Your Fats: The Complete Primer for Understanding the Nutrition of Fats, Oils, and Cholesterol.* Silver Springs, MD: Bethesda Press, 2000.

3 Omega Nutrition, www.omeganutrition.com

4 Vasant Lad, *Ayurveda: The Science of Self-Healing*, Santa Fe, NM: Lotus Press, 1984.

5
Smiling

The mind-body connection works both ways: there are things you can do with your body that change your feelings and your mind, and there are decisions made with your mind which change the body. Both directions can produce a sense of well being. This chapter is about smiling in the conventional sense and also about using your body in other ways to alter your thoughts and feelings.

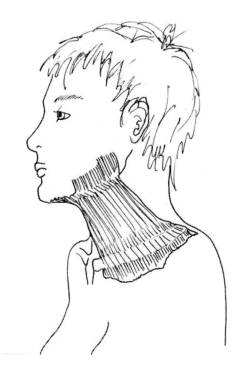

My father, a professional photographer, was very good at getting people to smile for the camera. He would tease, flirt and compliment, offering little stuffed animals and magic tricks. The only complaint I ever remember hearing from him about work was how hard it is to get some people to smile! If he was working today, I would suggest diffusing therapeutic-grade essential oils in his studio. Lavender, jasmine and rose are particularly uplifting.

Dad also used a "smile" command on us. After he cleaned a skinned knee or extracted a splinter, he invariably said, "Smile, it will make it feel better." If one of us kids had a particularly bad day, this is what we heard: "Be careful, that frown will freeze on your face. Smile."

-a young Denali

But good medicine is good medicine, and this prescription still works. Confused and grumpy, I put my face in a smile position, even though I'm not feeling the emotion to go with it (in fact, I'm feeling the very opposite emotion). When confronting a potential disaster on the physical, emotional or mental plane, a smile will give your heart enough room to think, helping your thoughts to avoid familiar ruts or dangerous leaps. As my then four-year-old daughter said in 1984, "You know Mom, our heart is the biggest brain we have in our body." Smiles are one way to access the biggest brain.

When you frown or are fearful, your diaphragm moves less than a quarter of an inch. When you feel neutral, your diaphragm contracts and expands more freely. And when you smile or experience pleasant thoughts, the diaphragm is capable of moving three to four inches. There appears to be a strong correlation

PLATYSMA

between perception of pleasantness and unpleasantness and the range of diaphragmatic movement even when you are simply impersonating those emotions rather than feeling them.[1]

When you smile, your soft palate rises and the back of your throat relaxes, creating more space. At the same time, more space opens in your chest for the heart, pericardium and diaphragm. I've observed one of my favorite teachers, Maria Nemeth, moving her face and jaw into a smile position as she works in her laboratory with groups of students, sharing her knowledge in word and action. When I practice the smile position, I discover a space beneath my heart that lights the way, as if my smiling mouth switches on a flashlight between the heart and the diaphragm. In cadavers, the space between heart and diaphragm is gone. In life, this space is available to help us face challenges.

Play with this smile movement for a moment before you fall asleep at night and in the morning before you get out of bed. Practice it before you enter a stressful situation, so you become aware of how it feels inside. Then try it out when you spot an impending jam, one that threatens to dissolve your balance. Mediators, judges and teachers might take smile breaks.

A small amount of physiological information is needed to understand the anatomy of the smile. The erect position of

humans means the pericardium (the outer sack covering the heart) needs strong superior attachments, or the heart would

be compressed in certain positions. Because the heart is so sta-
bilized by these ligaments, there is very little movement up
or down when the diaphragm descends to its flat inhalation
phase.

The heart hangs like a chandelier above the thoracic diaphragm. The pulmonary ligaments on both sides of the heart
attach the heart to the lungs, but stop an inch above the diaphragm. At rest, when we inhale, the soft palate and back of the
throat relax, as do other passages. Remember that on the inhalation, the diaphragm is flat-roofed, pouching the abdomen.
The diaphragm pulls down on the central tendon where the
pericardium, the sack of the heart, is attached. The diaphragm's
movement causes this sack to move lower than the heart, creating a gentle space when you inhale.

You can feel this. Take a breath and let it out, feeling deep
inside your chest, parallel to the tip of your sternum. Smile.
Breathe again. Feel the diaphragm make firmer contractions
into the abdomen, spreading your ribs to the sides like a bellows. The diaphragm, for most of your exhalation, is in a con-
trolled contraction, allowing for the "domed" muscle to move
up.

I believe that when you move your face into a smile that narrow space widens ever so slightly. You just felt the difference.
When your heart feels light as a feather or wide as the world,
your smile has something to do with it.   Ah, the genius of the
smile!

I also know the opposite to be true. A heavy heart translates
into squished space between the diaphragm and the heart. Your
diaphragm does not move much. Breathing is subdued, even
suppressed. The heart tires of being confined, and you grow
depressed. A light heart feels better, juicier, more alive. Your
heartstrings are tuned.

In the international code of anatomical drawings, yellow is
the color for nerves. As I look through my anatomy books, I

find myself mesmerized by a diagram of the nerves of the heart. The beautiful golden strings of nerves stretch elegantly from your head to your diaphragm. They call to mind a harp.

I think my young daughter was right: the heart is the biggest brain in your body. We particularly want our children to smile. Their well-being is our future.

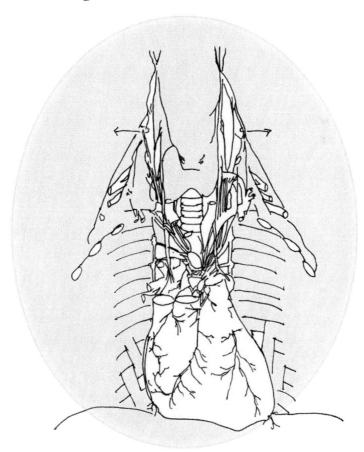

Other Body Positions. Besides smiling, there are a number of simple body positions that change your body chemistry and therefore your health. If these are not old sayings, they should be: "Sit up straight and attention will follow." "Put your hands together and God will listen." "Bow down to those you have oppressed and the seed of equality will be planted."

We celebrate spirit many ways. Prayer takes many forms. Around the world, morning and evening prayers happen every minute of our day. Whatever sacred name is used, however far away we are from each other in politics, complexion, ancestry, economics or individual experience of pain and pleasure, we are all praying to a universal life force. When my friend heard her life savings had been embezzled by her bank's president, she told me, "I got down on my knees and prayed." It made me recall how, as a young visitor to my great-grandmother's house, I saw her on her knees first thing upon rising and last thing before sleep, each and every day.

All of us have a cultural history of gathering together, even if it is just the annual singing of "Happy Birthday" as children. Several years ago a group of people from my village got together each month to share potluck and discuss a designated topic. I thought of it as an update to what my parents had called "Supper Club," a monthly party in someone's home with bridge following dinner. Dialogue was our "bridge." We shared our spiritual history. It was fascinating to listen to my respected friends tell tales of wandering, focus, embarrassment, innocence and desire to know spirit.

We were a mixed group. One woman started as an Episcopalian child, became a Baptist, then a Jehovah's Witness and is now a practicing Buddhist, clearly committed to the right of all to worship as they need. One man was raised in the stronghold of the Catholic Church: he still loves the theology, especially the teachings of Thomas Merton, and is now both a devout Buddhist and a pagan, keeping the holy holidays of all three traditions. Other friends' spiritual lineage included Jewish heritage (though not practice), a former Salvation Army soldier and a man who had died, was resuscitated, experiencing God.

One woman, an Air Force brat, grew up on bases where there were two churches, one labeled Catholic and the second,

"Other." At the age of forty, dining with her future in-laws, the hostess asked her to say grace. She punted with the one of two prayers she knew: bowing head, putting palms together, she said "Rub-a-dub-dub, thanks for the grub. Yay God!" No one objected. When you put your palms together, God listens.

To Stand Tall and Not Shrink. Inside your spine is a connective tissue called ligamentum flavum, yellow ligament. When it stays juicy and flexible, your spine is tall and healthy. To keep it so, try a forward bend with a little support under your butt from a blanket folded without wrinkles or uneven edges, and something in front of you to support your arms and

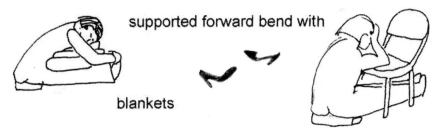

supported forward bend with

blankets

head. Evenly balanced on your blanket, extend your legs in front of you. Place a chair with the seat above your thighs or pile enough pillows and blankets on your lap and under your knees so you can lean forward resting your arms and head on the pile. You may find this easier if you start out with your back against the wall. When you lean forward, you will want to put a pillow between you and the wall. Your nervous system, intertwined in the muscles, likes to feel cradled.

To Cure Muscle Cramps. When your body complains of a cramp in your back or a stiff neck, it is important to find the most comfortable position that will allow you to rest. Temporary relief is one giant step in the direction of renewal. In essence, you intercept the neurological information from muscular pain by finding a comfortable supported position.

Many people mistakenly think that you fix a muscle cramp by stretching the muscle. But muscles by themselves do not stretch. Muscles can contract, hold or extend. What appears to be stretching is actually passive lengthening, responding to the contraction of opposing muscles called the "antagonist" muscles and the movement of bones. Help is often counterintuitive: when you're inclined to stretch a muscle out with massage and kneading, try instead to compress the cramping muscle. Let's take an example: you have been gardening for hours with new spring flowers, planting lovely rows of primrose and pansy. When you stand up, stretching, arching your back, you experience a cramp. Almost invariably, the muscles that cramp are those which were shortened for so long. In this case, the complainers are muscles on the inside of the spine, the ones opposite to the muscles that are being stretched by bending forward in the garden. Cramp isn't the ache of overuse, but an immediate, intense complaint from being scrunched too long in too-tight quarters without enough blood flow, creating a neuromuscular noose around bundles of muscle fiber.

To relieve your cramp, return to the position you were in for so long, on your hands and knees as you were gardening. Breathe in this compressed position for ninety seconds. Remember the "personal inch" explained in Chapter 1, The Sole of Being? Strongly press into the point you identified then, inch 5 on the inside of your arm opposite the side of the cramping side. Catch your breath. Slowly, very slowly, with the help of a chair, wheelbarrow, hoe or colleague, stand up. Be sure to take at least ninety seconds to assume a standing posture or the posture you were in when the cramp "struck"! You're almost certain to release your cramp.

Muscle Memory. Like your brains, your muscles sometimes get habituated to pain. It becomes their "normal" state, and you forget how it feels to relax. Forgetting how to relax the diaphragm is a major contributor to pain, suffering and maybe even stupidity. Collectively, we spend megabucks in pursuit of relief from the resulting symptoms and from the accelerated aging caused by forgetting how to relax. Stiffness, soreness and restricted range of motion are not natural, even though they may have become normalized in our culture. Constipa-

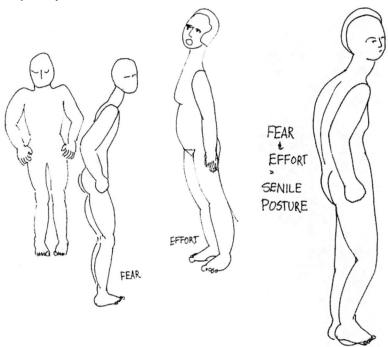

tion, insomnia, asthma, diabetes, cancer and heart disease are also not natural, though they may be all too normal because of our burdened environment, compromised exercise and depleted diet. It does not have to be this way.

Thomas Hanna, in his work with sensory–motor amnesia (SMA), spoke eloquently about the loss of memory in certain muscle groups. His work reintroduces consciousness to muscles. He identified three specific reflexes leading to habitual muscular contractions, calling them Red Light (or Fear), Green Light (or Effort) and Senile (the long duration of a combination of Fear and Effort).[2] He defined a series of movement to integrate the neurological muscular relationship. I like to start this daily developmental practice in bed. (Similar movements are found in other disciplines mentioned in this book: Pilates, Rosen, Alexander, Feldenkrais, yoga and Paula Garbourg's work with the sphincter muscles.)

1.

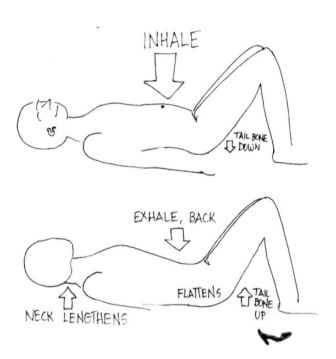

First Exercise. In bed, lie face up, without pillows unless your chin is higher than your forehead. Bend your knees so the soles of your feet are flat on the bed. Inhale, feeling your tailbone move toward the floor. Exhale, allowing your tailbone to tip toward the ceiling. As you inhale, your spine lengthens and extends; as you exhale, your spine curls forward and flexes. Repeat five times, slowly, observing your spinal movements.

2.

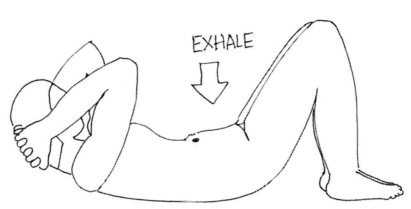

EXHALE

Second Exercise. On the last repetition of the previous exercise, interlace your fingers behind your head. Lift your head gently on the exhalation, rolling your belly over itself and flattening your back. Inhale as you release your head to the bed, bringing a slight arch into your spine. Repeat five times.

3.

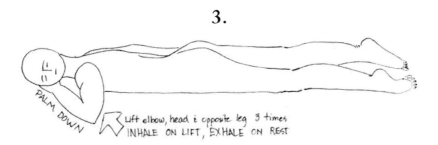

L
I
II
PALM DOWN
Lift elbow, head & opposite leg 3 times
INHALE ON LIFT, EXHALE ON REST

Third Exercise. Turn over on your stomach. With your head turned to the right, tuck your right hand under your left cheek. On a slow inhalation, lift your right hand and head as you also lift your left foot and leg. Inhale as you lift, exhale as you return to warm bedding. Moving slowly, repeat twice on one side, then switch to the other. This exercise arches your spine into an extension. It is gentle: it doesn't matter how much you lift, only that you cross over, moving opposite sides of the body at the same time. Feel where other body places want "to help." Don't go there. This movement often induces sleep.

4.

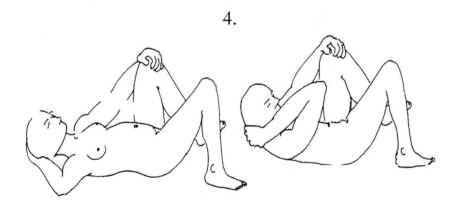

Fourth Exercise. Lie on your back with knees bent and spine relaxed, holding your left knee with your left hand. Then roll forward, exhaling, and lift your right elbow and head toward your left knee, flattening your back. Inhale as your back returns to the bed, arching your back into an extension. Repeat five times before you change sides.

5.

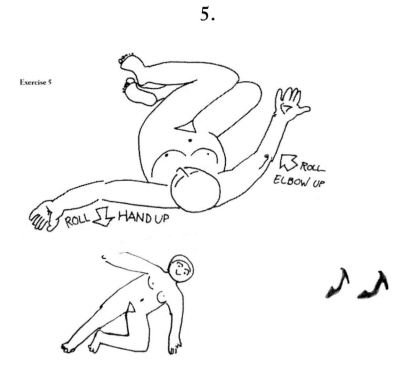

Exercise 5

ROLL ELBOW UP

ROLL HAND UP

Fifth Exercise. This movement is a twist. As in yoga, we warm up to twisting by extending and flexing the spine. Lying flat on your back, knees bent, palms up, extend your arms twelve inches away from your body. Drop your knees to the left, allowing your head to roll to the right. Breathe into your belly, feeling your twisting spine. Inhale, allowing your knees to roll to the right as your head rolls to the left. Repeat this gentle twist several times, feeling for subtle movements in your shoulders, elbows, hands and hips. Keeping the head opposite knee movement, on the "head" side, roll the arm and hand toward your head. You will see your little finger moving higher into the air and your thumb moving towards the floor. This is an external rotation of your shoulder. From your opposite shoulder, same side as your knees, roll your arm internally. This hand will move closer to your knees. Feel the movements through your spine. Repeat five times.

6.

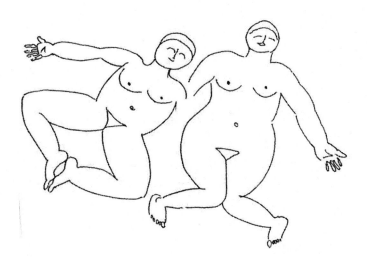

Sixth Exercise. Still lying on your back, keep your shoulders on the bed, legs extended. Draw your right heel as close as comfortably possible to your pelvic floor and tailbone. The outside of your right calf and right thigh slide along the floor or bed. This is an external rotation of the femur, your thigh. On an inhale, move the sole of your right foot to the floor/bed, bringing your right knee in line with the right side of your body. On an exhale, allow the bent right knee to move toward the midline of your body. Your right knee will cross on top of your left thigh. This is an internal rotation of the right femur. Slowly repeat the external and internal rotations five times. Please switch to the second side. Notice the movement in your lower back.

Finally, do both sides at the same time for five repetitions, bringing knees together and then them twisting apart. You are exaggerating knock-kneed and bowlegged movements.

7.

Seventh Exercise. Sit up, with knees facing the same direction in what I call the sorority girl photo pose. If your knees are to the left, place your right hand on your left shoulder. Gently twist to the left three times. Do not do this twist with your head, only your body. Now move your knees and hands to the opposite side and repeat. Dr. Hanna's version includes more eye and neck work. But for now, this will do.

Especially with age, there are many ways our bodies distort by repetitive pressures or simple misuse. Age and occupation often bring on bowlegs in men and knock-knees in women. Both the cowboy and the tall old lady regularly suffer distortion in the correct angle on the head of the femur—the trocanter—in the hip. In cowboys, the angle gets larger, meaning that, for balance, the knees have to compensate by moving outward; this is called valgus. In older women, the angle gets smaller, compelling the femurs to move closer together, creating knee collision, called varus. The normal angle for your hipbone is 125 degrees. The knock-knees typical of old age produce 110 degrees, and on a

bowlegged cowboy, the angle is 145 degrees.

These gentle exercises will help to keep your hip joints flexible and in position. If you add them to the belly bolster exercises I recommended in Chapter 3, Buddha Full Belly, and the cat and dog tilts on all fours I described in Chapter 2, Diaphragms, you'll stay limber, like a smart animal caring for herself for the long term. My valentine to myself each year is starting each day with these lovely undercover lifts and twists, followed by three pairs of cat stretches and tilted dogs. Join me, won't you?

Smiling With Your Mind. No one fully understands the extent to which the mind can control the body, but it appears to be extreme. For example, highly adept yogis or siddhas have been shown to be impervious to pain or injury, exposing themselves to fire and other dangers without affecting their bodies in the slightest. The spiritual teacher Ram Dass recounted stories of his guru ingesting enough LSD to unhinge a normal human mind. The guru exhibited absolutely no effects.

All of us know people who expect the worst and reliably get it. The question is, if such a person could train herself to expect the best, would her body respond? I believe so. Sometimes I see clients who are mired in misery, whose despair is intractable. I ask them this: "Who do you want to win this argument? Right now, I'm more on your side than you are." If they are willing to save their own lives, I invite them to do this: "Humor me," I say, "for just ten minutes, pretend life is good. Pretend you're getting better. Let yourself enter fully into this awareness, let every cell enter this reality." If the client takes a breath that is a sigh of relief, I know he or she has stepped across the brain boundary between despair and possibility.

The future encompasses multiple possibilities. We can never know which will unfold. As with your face and heart, smiling with your mind calls the cosmic healers.

Notes

1 Takahi Nakamura, *Oriental Breathing Therapy*, Tokyo, Japan: Japan Publications, Inc., 1981 pp. 13-15.

2 Thomas Hanna, *Somatic: Reawakening the Mind's Control of Movement, Flexibility and Health*. Reading, MA: Addison-Wesley, 1988.

6
Listening

*Only those who have the patience to do
simple things perfectly will acquire the
skill to do difficult things easily.*

—Johann von Schiller

Learning to listen. Years ago a shaman came to town.
My colleagues encouraged me to spend time with this wild
man. "He will teach you, Darca," they said. The previous year,
an epidemic of a strange, viral-like disease had appeared in
North Lake Tahoe at Incline Village.   From reports, victims
suffered fatigue, pains and headaches leading to severe depression. Other cases were reported elsewhere, but no one knew a
treatment. That spring the Centers for Disease Control had just
recognized EBV, Epstein-Barr Virus as a disease, rather than
simply dismissing it as bad attitude.[1] Sufferers were desperate:
"I don't care what I have, just help me!" One of those sufferers
was a close friend. So I was further enticed by promises that the
shaman knew how to heal difficult and rare diseases.

The shaman traveled the world by the grace of benefactors.
Like most shamans, he lived outside the rules, telling whatever stories pleased him or served his purposes. Shamans often
change everyone else's plans. This shaman was no different. His
arrival in life was a case in point: his mother, traveling cross-

country via airplane, went into labor, requiring an unscheduled touchdown in Kansas City, Missouri.

The shaman's teacher was an ancient woman who appeared to be twenty. At intervals, the shaman departed the area, saying he needed to unearth the witch, pulling her out of darkness. She was able to look twenty years old in a hundred-year-old body by being buried in the dark for part of each month.[2]

Hearing all this, I was curious but cautious. This man was not someone I was inclined to hang with but knowledge has a way of arriving in challenging packages. Toothless, with glistening hair, he had a slippery legal history involving drugs and dark dealings, and an air of "cool" streetwise scrawniness. A friend who knew him during the drugs and dark period wanted to know what happened to make him grow beautiful hair, he was such a sleaze when she knew him. At the time, I didn't know the answer to that question.

Starting in late spring, we scheduled a month of weekly day long sessions. For the first outing we headed south, twelve miles. I drove. He directed.

We parked north of our destination and walked across the railroad bridge to the other side of the river, moving away from the highway through warm, fragrant spring air. The green glowing new leaves and new life along the river was so thick and vibrant, a juicy lightness took the edge off my misgivings, priming me for adventure. As we reached a straight, level stretch of rail, the shaman instructed me to take off my hiking shoes and socks. "Leave them." He pointed to the side of the track. "We'll be back this way."

The number one rule of earthquake preparedness: know where your shoes are. The number one rule of physical safety: wear good shoes. *Oh, great,* I thought, *I am off to the wilderness, leaving my shoes to the bears and the bees and who knows what other creatures?*

"Think I'll just tie 'em around my neck," I said.

"Okay. Your exercise is to walk one hundred feet on this track, barefoot, blindfolded. If you fall off, start again."

To walk a hundred feet, I thought, *I can put my shoes down.* For more than an hour, I practiced taking one small step after another, gradually increasing the time I remained on track before my chattering brain caused me to lose balancing breath and step off onto railway ties or crushed rock.

Blessed with long toes, I learned to wrap them around the edge of the beam for support and balance. The shaman suggested I was cheating. He then left me alone, going farther down the tracks to lie on the ties and nap.

I was glad to be inches above ground level rather than on a high balance beam, as falling off every few feet would have been much more trying. The sun heated the iron hotter than the surroundings. My feet began to ache. Suddenly, I heard rumblings and felt vibrations through my feet. Taking off my blindfold, I watched the local track repair crew approach in a four-person gondola. I shouted to the sleeping shaman. The suggestion that his headrest might involve his beheading was perhaps a sign. He declared that I had completed enough of the hundred feet to pass the first test.

Rock Climbing. Rising abruptly out of fast-moving water, the formation looked to my Iowa eyes more like a mountain than a rock. But I knew enough of rock climbing to understand this volcanic formation is considered "shit" by climbers. Volcanic rock is unstable, loose, easily displaced. It is not the elegant granite of Yosemite or the Grand Tetons, Nature's natural ladders. If you are to be one with the elements, choose your elements wisely.

"No" I said. "I am not climbing this stuff. It gives way. I have a three-year-old daughter at home who needs me." Cat quick, he started up the rock beside the 150-year-old railroad tunnel timbers. Thirteen feet up rock gave way under his weight.

Only his fingers held an edge. Pushing away from the wall, he jumped with a twist, landing on all fours. A trickle of stones dribbled after him.

What next? "Take me out to dinner," he said as he dusted himself off. "We'll do the barefoot run through the woods another day. You are lucky I'm hungry." He ate. I was too tired from my hot foot afternoon to do more than sit there and then pay the bill.

On the second outing, a lovely spring day, I made a barefoot run on soft grasses through the woods, contacting heavenly earth. My feet did fine. Instructions went well. By assigning me rigorous, simple tasks in nature, he taught me listening with my body. I learned to listen to the energy, to feelings of heat, wind and cold on particular areas of my body. I listened to colors as they pulsed in spring light, listened to my body alone and in relationship with birds, plants, the land, the earth body constantly interacting with my body.

Parallel to my rigorous outside nature training, my friend with Epstein-Barr Virus commenced an intensive "inside" natural detoxification. This took six months but he subsequently recovered.

Listening With the Sense of Sounds. Years ago, Claude Steiner, PhD, a psychotherapist, told me that if he had to lose one of his senses, the one he would most resist giving

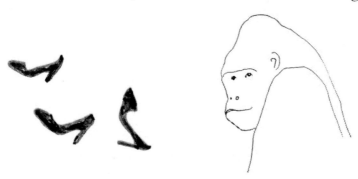

up was hearing.[3] He could keep doing his analytic work as long as he could hear. Even if taste, smell, sight and touch vanished, he'd be happy to work, listening to content but hearing the sounds of the stories tell the truth of the tale.

"Seamless," is how an actress I know described her ten-day experience of silent Vipassana meditation.[4] In a seamless condition, past and present flow in perpetual interconnection. Listening, observing breath, aches and pains — as well as joys and comforts — arise and pass away, proclaiming the truth of the Universe: this too shall pass.

I have found listening engages seamlessness faster than any other sense. Every organ and organism serves in ways known and unknown. The ancient trees of northern Californian, Siberian and Amazonian forests soothe the wind, tease the rain, temper solar storms and summer heat, ground earthborne viruses, bacteria and molds, thus keeping a lid on Pandora's box of disease. Have you heard the morning cry of the crow and blue jay replacing the music of our edible, delectable, vanishing songbirds? Listening deeply, we detect a sound shift forewarning us of changes we are causing in species populations. Listen carefully, for like the women of Troy, Rosa Parks, and students in the 'sixties, the marching children have much to say about the new world order: equality and equanimity are intimately connected.

Listening With Touch.

Often we listen with our fingertips and hands. Osteopaths diagnose by using their hands to listen to a patient. "When a particular tissue is ill," write Jean Barral and Pierre Mercier, "it loses its elasticity, disrupts   the patient's membranous equilibrium, and becomes a new axis or pivot point for the motions of mobility and motility."[5] The wisdom of these gifted teachers and healers serves all of us. When using your hands to heal, you must wait, listening with your body for dysfunctional areas, pain or congestion. If you listen quietly, these areas draw your hands to them. They need you to touch them. They need your movement, your touch. These areas are without movement. When listening, pay attention to the first motion, the first little ripple or pulse or slight sigh. This is the truth of life. Life is motion.

Keep your hands passive, searching for soft tissue tension to talk to you. Inhale while listening. Relax your shoulders. Focus on the tissue under your hands, your touch. Feel your fingers relax. Collect information from your friend by listening for her breath, connective tissue motion, pulse. If you cannot hear your friend's breath, pulse, connective tissue, listen for your breath, pulse, connective tissue motion. Go back and forth, between your inside awareness and observing your friend. Somewhere between you and your friend, you will hear the beat, feel her rhythm of motion from both your friend's and your own body. Observe how your listening hands help your own body relax, lending movement to the relationship between you and your friend.

Listening With Breath. In difficult therapeutic situations, I copy the rhythm of my client's breathing pattern, sharing with my body a few moments of her respiration. During the quiet, trance time of massage meditation, I feel the habitual rhythm with which she receives the world. This is similar to getting the pitch or key of a song, getting in step with the marching band or dancing the tango. Breathe together. Listening with the breath and for the breath, you hear sighs of relief as muscles unwind, arterial flows relax, tendons and ligaments soften. You can do this in any setting. Lovely sighs at the table are songs of satisfaction. Contentment after a fabulous meal compliments the chef. Similar sounds of delicious satisfaction come with sensually sharing pleasures, making oxytocin, the hormone of tend and befriend. Oxytocin, the hormone of satisfaction, easily generated by touch from massage or lovemaking also comes from doing that which *pleases* you.

Listening With the Body. While I work, body sounds give me clues, enabling me to discern what is being released. Rumbling sounds made by gas in the alimentary tract, are a marvelous way to hear the body relaxing, releasing tensions. There is the rumbling grumbling of an empty stomach. There is the gurgle of the belly bolster moving gas and fluids around the colon. As a massage client relaxes, sounds I listen for are valves "taking a breath," letting off steam. Touch and breath purge internal tissue tension from the gossamer network within connective tissue and muscle. You've heard those internal sighs. All of these "soundings" are considered *borborygmus*, one of my favorite medical terms.

Under a blanket on the treatment table, my friend lies on her side, knees bent, head on a pillow. The afternoon sun pours through the west window curtains of the treatment room.

We are back to back. She is horizontal, reclining. I am vertical, standing. I gently lower a percentage of my weight, leaning with my forearm and elbow onto her waist. She rolls forward, away from me, moving the pain out of her muscles. Her abdomen starts singing borborygmus from all quadrants. She laughs, "What a relief. The sides feel better." The kinks have given up, releasing gas and fluids.

Body Listening is Different for Each of Us. Some people listen with colors: certain types of music sound purple, others yellow. Neurologists call this synesthesia. Even those of us without this gift can listen in color. A group of friends planned a quilting retreat with this assignment: each was to create an artistic rendition of her vagina. They spend the weekend retreat vision questing their stories from the sacred womb of their own vaginas, sharing their stories and sewing. They returned home bearing quilts splashed red, royal blue and purple, with scraps

PLEASE GENTLY ROLL FORWARD.

GENTLE PRESSURE into the External Oblique muscles.

of black lace or soft pink gloves for labia. All created fantastic worlds of color and texture. All were wildly different. All this creative diversity arose from one weekend trip into vaginal life stories!

Other people listen with light. One old friend is a sensor of light and seer of energy, not in a "New Age" psychic sense, but like Monet, Vermeer, Turner. Traveling with him, listening to his description of light in the valley, on the sea, around someone's eyes, I realize light is his natural element. I recognize his language of listening for health and well-being must revolve around illumination.

Simple sensation. Sometimes I feel in my body what is happening in your body. The presence of energy is the easiest way to describe the sensations filtering into my body as I pass my hand over your body. As I pass my hand over your body, I am reminded of the way my grandfather used his finger to read down each page of his newspaper, speaking softly to himself. As I slowly float my left hand above your body, I report changing sensations in my own body. I feel lightness and weight, fullness and emptiness, steadiness and fluctuation, coolness and warmth. These feelings and sensations tap my muscles or settle deep into extracellular space. I gather information, using both hands, one hand two or three feet above the body, the other hand to the side of the massage table, gently sandwiching tissue and space. As your energy fields change, the changes are projected onto the screen of my body. How may I serve you? Heart listening with hands, breathing into diaphragmatic floors, loving your willingness to present your natural beauty, I mirror your strength, receive your weakness and acknowledge your task: loving all your body, all yourself.

This was how the shaman taught me, instructing me to move my hands in both directions, head to toe and toe to head, switching hands. Moving slowly, observing, breathing, sensing, body listening. Just as a deaf person perceives communication clues—reading lips, feeling vibrations, recognizing familiar topics, alert for differences and similarities—I am open to information. Grounded at my base, I feel who you are in this moment, repeating this body listening at the end of our session. Your body and words, sounding your energy, tell me the truth in the beginning of our hour. The silence and sensation tell me the truth at the end of our hour.

Listening Stance. The most powerful way to listen is from a stance of not-knowing. When you are willing to suspend knowing, leaping into the unknown, trusting the universe to hold us in her arms, you create the most powerful listening stance possible. In contrast, nibbling away at listening, coming to the encounter with preconceived ideas about what is supposed to happen, undermines your ability to hear deeply.

Warriors Listen. Virabhadrasana I, Warrior One, and Virabhadrasana II, Warrior Two, are basic standing yoga poses. They are for everyone, generals and commanders, little old ladies and wimps. Do battle inside yourself, winning the war of words. Be silent. Observe. Hold each pose with dignity and comfort, enjoying the rhythmic sounds from your breath.

Listening deeply begins in silence. Stop talking for a day or a week. Listen to the internal conversation in your head until you are sick of repeating your grumpy, frightened and frightening self. Watch your self-created pains pass by: now indignant, now self-justifying, now blaming others for discomfort, now pointing fingers. Take time to notice that each time you point at another for causing your pain, three fingers point back at you. Get bored enough to be quiet. Listening is one way out of the repetitive cycle of self-created emotional pain. Place the tip of your tongue on the inside of your upper front teeth. Relax your shoulders. Listen for your breath.

Listening to Content. Years ago I observed a psychologist research propaganda. Joseph Goebbels, Hitler's Propaganda Minister, is considered one of the most effective propagandists in history. Using the skills and tools of an advertising industry, this Nazi sold the world on fascism, becoming the master of Hitler's "great lie . . . the sound principle that the magnitude of a lie always contains a certain factor of credibility, since the great masses of the people in the very bottom of their hearts tend to be corrupted rather than consciously and purposely evil, and that therefore, in view of the primitive simplicity of their minds, they more easily fall victim to a big lie than to a little one."[6] This truth-to-lie ratio continues to be used on us every day. Listen carefully to the whole sentence. Stay present in your warrior stance.

Another powerful tool of propaganda is the metaphor, a figure of speech in which a word or phrase denoting one kind of object or action is used in place of another, suggesting a likeness or analogy between them. Metaphors are great for poets and power moguls. These "as if" expressions can tap into fears: free the slaves and the slaves will swarm over us like locusts. Such words can be used to draw our deepest fears to the surface, amplifying ordinary pain into horror: "You dragged me through the dirt, cut me off at the knees and stabbed me in the back." None of these is literally true; each exaggerates the truth it masks. Listen closely to content. Listen clearly for descriptions. Be aware of metaphor; don't let them slide silently into your subconscious.

There is a little voice inside you, guarding, encircling your energy field. Listen for her. She alerts us in dreams, plants reminders in chance encounters, speaks through your best friend's mouth.

Listen to the Way You Name Things. Dr. Ellerbroek says, "We, as human beings, have long been noted to have a tendency to believe that our personal name for a thing is the 'right' name. Although this appears on the surface to be a fairly harmless behavior, it is not, since it tends to produce closure. For example, we doctors seem to have a predilection for nouns in naming disease, for example: *epilepsy, measles, brain tumors,* and because these conditions 'deserve' nouns as names, then obviously they are things to us."[7]

Use as many action words as possible. Describing living, changing conditions often opens the doors to healing faster than using nouns—fixed conditions which attempt to pinpoint and control the uncontrollable. Noun addictions empower "conditions" and disease. The disease has a life of its own: The cancer just took her away. My heart attack defines the way I see the world. A noun addiction often takes our thinking hostage: I am a heart disease victim, a cancer victim, a stroke victim. The disease literally occupies space in our bodies, our minds, our emotions, and our spirits, disrupting our presence and power.

Certainly, these situations—cancer, diabetes, heart disease—involve change. Life is different. Life is always different. Change opens the door to miracles. If we tie an anchor, a sentence, around a health situation, the results are often "battling," "fighting" an enemy rather than engaging in healing.

In modern medicine, some of these diseases have become deities, worshipped by entire industries. Like the ancient gods demanding blood sacrifice, we might sacrifice the patient for the sake of research or insurance reimbursement. If today my friend announces an inexpensive, easily available cure for cancer the impact on our economy would likely be as great as the sub-prime mortgage or credit card meltdown. For example, we know after more than thirty years of hormone replacement therapy (HRT) some women do well on HRT, some women get cancer on HRT—and some women don't need HRT. [8]

In contrast to the recommendations of doctors in years past, not all women, at all times, need hormone replacement therapy. Women do not fit a singular situation.

How we name things has a huge impact on the way we see them. The other day a client informed me that his "liver and pancreas shut down" after a long sickness. "Stop using that description!" I counseled. "If your liver and pancreas were shut down, we would be burying you. How do your hardworking liver and pancreas feel about the way you refer to their contribution to your health? Even though you are not enjoying optimal strength, you are certainly far from under the ground."

When we tell the truth of our experience, we speak of sensation: pain, empathy, sounds of grunting and groaning. Try to speak accurately for a day. Give up the jargon for a week. As Kipling said, "Words are, of course, the most powerful drug used by mankind."[9] Jargon is addictive. It will make you lazy. Precision with our words in messy places keeps us conscious, slows us down, teaches us real power.

Listening to What We Ask For. Remember this old story? A devout woman prays every day for guidance from God. She is caught in a flood. Her house is surrounded by water. The TV and radio warn folks in her neighborhood to move to safer ground. She doesn't leave. Sirens sound. She doesn't leave. The water rises so high, it forces her onto the roof of her house. A rescue boat arrives, but she will not leave, declaring, "God will save me." A helicopter arrives, but she will not leave.

The woman drowns and goes to heaven. She says to God, "I prayed to you every day of my life. You did not help me. I wanted you to rescue me." "What?" he says, "who do you think sent the TV and radio warnings, the sirens, the rescue boat and the helicopter?" She died because she could not get past the messenger. She stopped listening to what she had asked for!

Listening to Pain. There are many kinds of pain. All pain evokes unconscious and conscious physical, emotional, mental and spiritual reactions. All pain sensations inform.

Through breath and focus, information comes to you. My friend, a health care practitioner and artist, hurt her foot. No big deal, she thought, she knew how to manage: rest, ice, compress, elevate—the "RICE" formula for strains. A few days later she drew a picture of her resting foot. The drawing showed a thin line through the heel, the area that hurt. It looked as if she had broken a bone. Since her foot continued to hurt, she decided to get an X-ray. Viola! The picture revealed a tiny break uncannily similar to her drawing.

In my yoga classes, I prefer to work progressively from gentle movements toward more intense positions. "Listen to the conversation with your hips, calves, abdominal muscles." I instruct as we sustain nontraumatizing poses. My college baseball pitchers, middle-aged martial artists and soon-to-be little old ladies make the same sounds as we extend calf muscles, rotate hips and slide shoulder blades laterally. Little mutters, breath moving, moans and groans escape everyone at one time or another. Listening is another path to beauty and health.

Listening Anew to an Old Story. Most of us humans tie ourselves up with personal stories set in cement: called by some "thought forms" or "scripts" when the thought objects are strung together to define one's life.[10] One healing act of listening involves revisiting a story which has shaped your life, hardening into thought object/script tough as reinforced concrete. The subject can be trivial or singularly important. One friend says, "I never wear black. I don't look good in it." This thought-object/script takes precedence over the fact that she looks absolutely smashing in black.

Listening anew opens consciousness, good medicine for all parts of our bodies: heart, head, gut, hands and feet. When I revisit a family story, I listen with all of my body, sensing both highlights and dark places in my physical, emotional, mental and spiritual bodies.

For example, I inherited a lofty story of love that I carried as a thought object/script for most of my life, shaping my ideas about romance and relationship. With hindsight and healings, I recognized relationship disconnections—not evil or violent—but blindness which disrupted my sense of healthy relationships.

My mother's mother, Marie, was diagnosed with a damaged heart weeks before my mother found out she was pregnant with me. As I was coming into being en utero, Marie was dying in the world. She died at forty-nine, during surgery to amputate her gangrenous leg.

Marie was legendary. Strangers told me stories of her independence, fierceness and fineness. "Oh, you're Otto's granddaughter and Marie's," they would say. "Bless her. Let me tell you the time she took us sledding on the north forty," or swimming or ice skating or played a funny trick on the hired hand who came home drunk.

She was life, people said: strong, imaginative, powerful and clear. She directed my grandfather. He worshipped her. They must have laughed a lot. From the stories, she was ageless. Their love was ideal. It is hard for me to imagine daily struggles or disagreements between them. She must have been lenient, yet firm. When my grandfather wanted to go to Montana to buy more land, she said, "No, there is only so much land one man needs."

Their love was a love of legend, always from the mouths and hearts of those who knew her. I remember my grandfather's tone of longing and deep sadness, still missing the beloved, even after years of marriage to a good woman who was not his Marie. Now, after more than half a century, I am ready to dismantle my thought object/script about lofty love.

The only person I do not remember telling stories about Marie was her mother, my great-grandmother, Dora Sibley.

My throat tightens like a tourniquet when I think of her, chok-
ing back a howl of torment coming from a thousand years of
mothers crying for their dead children. Dora lost both of her
children. Baby Stanley died shortly after birth and Marie died
when Dora was seventy. How does a great-grandmother speak
to her five-year-old great-granddaughter about the daughter
she outlived?

I don't remember Dora ever trying. If I imagine such a conversation, it might be in the afternoon after tea and chocolate
cake with brown burnt sugar frosting. A fresh glass of milk
would sit by my plate. My handsome Uncle Stanley, Marie's son,
would have stopped by for a piece of cake, leaving
behind two gallon- sized metal cans, one of
honey and the other of fresh whole milk.

We would be sit- ting in overstuffed rockers,
watching diffuse after- noon sunlight on the Afri-
can violets. I would be trying to reconstruct the family order. I
have a grandma, Clara, Grandpa's second wife. That was how
they always said it: Clara was always known as Otto's second
wife, as if order were important, almost as the Chinese confer
first wife, second wife and third wife status. As I see myself sitting there, listening becomes visceral. Information about relationships settles into my young mind. Clara stays home, I know,
doing what Grandpa asks, frying food and baking bread. She
has a dry sense of humor. Some days, I see little twinkles in
both Clara's and Grandpa's beautiful blue eyes, but mostly it
seems to be an "old" relationship, even though it is newer than
I am.

From what I can see, romance died with Marie. After her
death, Grandpa was beside himself for a year. I heard he left
home, but how could this be, since he had a fourteen-year-
old son who needed a father? A year later, he returned with a
new bride. Clara was a proper widow with Lutheran commit-
ments, but many years earlier, she had been Grandpa's first date.

Theirs was a northwest Iowa mixed marriage: they go to separate churches, Congregational and Lutheran, unless Grandpa has church at home, putting his feet up and tuning into the Sunday morning radio worship service.

The last thing Marie said to Otto before going into surgery was, "I've raised the girl. You raise the boy." My relatives said she would not have been happy in a wheelchair, without legs to take her skating. They said it was a matter of time until her heart, weakened by rheumatic fever, would stop working, even with the gangrenous leg amputated. The doctors at the Mayo Clinic in 1948 said this: "Take her home. Make her happy. There is nothing we can do for her damaged heart."

So my grandfather built his version of the Taj Mahal, a palace to his love: a log cabin cottage on Lost Island Lake, a few miles from their farm. The cabin was completed in the spring. She died that fall. How do I hear this story now? How did I hear the sounds then?

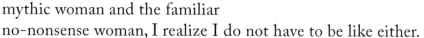

I am thankful for the image of creative, courageous, playful Marie. I am grateful for the experience of seeing my grandmother, Clara, with my grandfather, Otto, as a stable couple. Integrating the exciting mythic woman and the familiar no-nonsense woman, I realize I do not have to be like either.

Besides acting or reacting to personal scripts and thought forms, I've lived through an era of "Free Love" which was not free, the rise of sexually transmitted diseases, a wave of feminism and liberation as well as a backlash so violent I can only hope that the lash is the last gasp of patriarchal tyrants void of heart and wisdom. I do know my own freedom is inextricably tied to the well-being and health of the rest of the world: female and male, two legged and four, feathered and finned, vertebrate and invertebrate, foliaged, firma and oceanic.

Like the belief that mythic love is in one body and every-day practical partnership in another body, other thought forms/scripts are deeply stored, their power eluding me. With deep listening and quiet observation I recognize outdated, dead-ly thought forms/scripts affecting my health, bank account, friendships, creativity, time and spiritual development. For me to courageously confront what is not happy and healthy about my life, listening is one of the most powerful tools toward recovery.

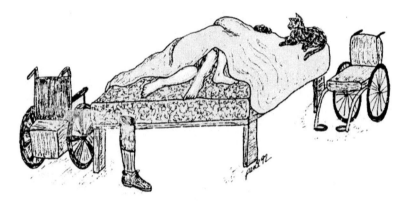

– Peni Hall, 1992

What stories have too long shaped your life? What stories need to be revisited with kindness and generosity? Where do you listen easily or ignore information? In your physical body? In your emotional body? Your intellectual body? Your spiritual body? Bodily lines merge like colors of the rainbow. Energetic particles in and around us know the effects of binding scripts and thought forms.

Think lovingly of yourself and hear yourself say sweet things about your beauty. All of us are familiar with "romantic" por-traits, all dewy and misty-eyed. Look at yourself through those eyes: gaze in the mirror by candlelight, focusing on an area of your body that serves you well. Note what it is you like and love about this strong, sleek, voluptuous form. Notice other women, note their "beauty marks," those attributes you find most attractive. All of my friends are beautiful and healthy in some way. Listen to your friends tell you how beautiful you are. Believe them. Let them be your coaches.

Years ago when I started this writing project, I read a manual by Allen and Ellie DeEver entitled: *How to Write a Book on Anything in Two Weeks or Less: Total Writing Concept 2000.*[11] It suggested we ask five friends what they liked about us. Using the Internet, the instant response I received was overwhelming. It was as if I were listening to my most wonderful eulogies. If you have yet to hear what five of your dear friends like about you, go girl—ask them now. It's the best gift ever. If the words come to you in written form, read them out loud or have a friend read these love letters to you. Unparalleled nutrition for the spirit.

Listening to Yourself. No is no and yes is yes. When someone asks you to do something and you say, "I'll try" or "maybe," you are really saying "no" but buying time, asking for inside listening space to confirm your initial response.

Utter an enthusiastic "yes." Listen to how your body hears you say "yes." If there is any hesitation, ask yourself whether you have second thoughts. Notice if you are surprised by your thoughts, if you are feeling "yes" where you expected "no" or vice versa. These are all acts of listening at deeper levels, giving yourself space to hear your own voice inside your gut, heart and soul. Layers of information in yourself and the world are revealed as you practice listening with more of your being.

Often, we say yes to please others, without considering the

cost to ourselves. Most of us long to be cared for the way we care for others. You can start by giving yourself and others the gift of saying, "No, I cannot do this today," when that is the deeper truth. Service is a choice; slavery is not. The freedom to change your mind is a sign of maturity.

Spread Your Listening Net. A local professional committed to a nonprofit regularly signs and sends letters requesting donations. In his personal life he seldom carries a checkbook. As we finish an appointment he reminds me that he will drop a check by. This takes a couple of weeks, involves several messages and checking the drop site. The continued energy field of our exchange speaks to me. I suggest that sluggish financial support for the nonprofit relates directly to his personal sluggish financial response to outstanding debts. Might one small change of paying for services immediately influence the wealth of the organization? Listen to what you ask to receive in one area of your life. What and how you ask to receive stands next to what and how you give. Diplomatic reciprocity, or do unto others, works inside and outside our bodies, minds, emotions and spirits. It is well worth integrating into our daily lives. Cleaning, clearing, informing and supporting one health arena effects the other arenas of your life.

Almost all mistakes are rooted in not listening. For example, when we feel abandoned—when we are overtaken by panic, separation and loneliness—we are not listening to our connections to the safety net of the universal life force simmering inside our bodies. When you listen, you connect. When you connect, you are not abandoned. Neither baby bears nor baby humans survive true physical abandonment in the first three years of life. If you are alive as an adult, you were not physically abandoned as a child. You might not have been treated well, you might have been treated horribly, tortured and abused. But you are here today, still capable and gifted. It may take enormous amounts of work and play to shed thought forms and scripts but the gift of a human body houses power capable of transforming a curse anyone else has perpetrated on you. It takes courage to step beyond familiar pain. You are truly a miracle. You can perform miracles. You can feel good, behave in a straight-up way and heal yourself and others.

There are many factors affecting health and disease. Certainly this book deals with individual choices and attitudes. But ancestry, environment, economics, location, and sheer luck-of the-draw also determine health. Massive sperm teamwork allows one sperm to order your state. The Sanskrit "karma" is an ancient concept describing the burden one carries from a past life into the present in order to become conscious. The ancients believed all forces effectively developed karma (from the season in which you were conceived to the history of your actions). It is now commonly used to denote the results of patterns formed by actions, patterns shaping one's life. In New Age parlance, we earn "good karma" in the benefits of right action, or "bad karma" when our actions bring much sadness and pain. As Ellen Cannon Reed says, "Karma means 'evolution,' not retribution. Karmic lessons are spiritual lessons."[12]

What if, in fact, "karma" is a collective opportunity to experience all of life's potential realities? What if, because we collectively allow poverty and torture—by tacit agreement, if not overt action—universal law required each one of us and all our loved ones a lifetime rotation into all experiences, horrific or happy? Would you allow girls to be pimped into prostitution in Pakistan, India or the United States if you knew you were dooming yourself to that very same human rights abuse in your next lifetime?[13] Would you allow bombs to be dropped on innocent families? Would you allow Kurdistan to be enveloped in nerve gas and mustard gas? Would you allow torture if you knew your loved ones were the next generation in line for the same experiences? I believe this is a truth: if an experience exists in this world, we receive it somewhere, somehow.

When you set your mind to stillness, to listening, you are enormously powerful. I want to close with a statement from Laurens van der Post on the responsibility this entails: "In every human situation there is a great responsibility laid on all of us by life that the person who is most aware, most highly, most completely, most widely conscious in a situation of conflict must accept responsibility for the person who is less conscious, who is possessed."[14]

Notes

1 Epstein-Barr Virus Disease (EBV) June, 2007, the Centers for Disease Control and Prevention released studies linking EBV to genetic mutations and abnormalities in gene expression involving key physiological processes.

2 There are several ancient traditions of "dark retreats": Tibetan, Mayan, and Siddha Vaidya, called Kayakalpa.

3 Claude Steiner, PhD, Bay Area Radical Therapy Collective, Berkeley, CA: Issues in Radical Therapy. 1974-1984. www.emotional-literacy.com

4 Vipassana, www.dharma.org

5 Jean-Paul Barral, DO and Pierre Mercier, DO, *Visceral Manipulation I.* Seattle, WA: Eastland Press, Inc., 1988.

6 Adolf Hitler, *Mein Kampf.* Munich, Ger: Eher-Verlag 1926

7 W.C. Ellerbroek, MD, "Language, Thought & Disease." *Perspectives in Biology and Medicine*, vol. 16, no 2. Winter 1973.

8 www.breastcancer.org

9 Rudyard Kiping. Quote attributed to R.K. in London Times 1923.

10 Eric Berne, MD, proposed that dysfunctional behavior is the result of self-limiting decisions made in childhood in the interest of survival. Such decisions culminate in what Berne called the "life script," the preconscious life plan that governs the way life is lived out. Changing the life script is the aim of transactional analysis psychotherapy. Replacing violent organizational or societal scripting with cooperative nonviolent behavior is the aim of other applications of transactional analysis. www.itaa-net.org.

11 Allen DeEver & Ellie DeEver, *How to Write a Book on Anything in Two Weeks or Less*. Reno, NV: Lightspeed Book Publishers, Inc. ,1998.

12 Ellen Cannon Reed, *Witches Quabala the Pagan Path and the Tree of Life*. York Beach, ME: Samuel Weiser, Inc. 1997.

13 Prostitution Research & Education is a San Francisco non-profit organization whose aim is to expand public awareness about the harms of prostitution/trafficking. Projects include a cross-cultural study of men who buy people in prostitution, with the goal of preventing prostitution. www.prostitutionresearch.com

14 Mickey Lemle, *Hasten Slowly,* a film about the life of Sir Laurens van der Post, Lemle Pictures, 1997.

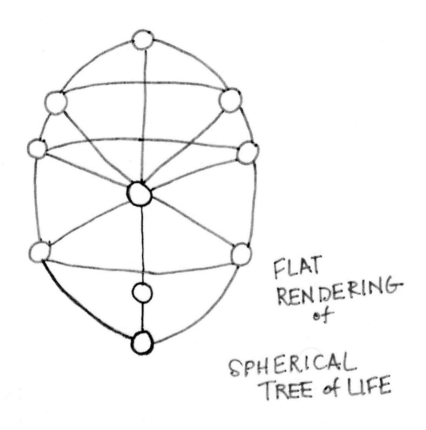

FLAT RENDERING of

SPHERICAL TREE of LIFE

7

Mix Your Medicines

One adage of my childhood was "do not mix medicines," but as far as I could see, no one ever respected that rule. Both my grandparents and my great-grandparents had overflowing medicine cabinets, supplementing them with standing medicine chests tucked into bathroom corners. The kitchen pantry and refrigerator shelves—not to mention the garden—held numerous substances for whatever ailed you. We used a poultice of clay for insect bites. We took ginger ale or the blue bottle of milk of magnesia for the tummy; an aspirin for muscle aches and bruises, and hearty beef broth, sore throat lozenges and used the vaporizer and Vicks Vapo-Rub for colds. No matter what your complaint, there were always two or three remedies to set you right.

Years later, as a work-study student at the University of Iowa School of Pharmacy, I coded for the groundbreaking, federally funded, computerized Unit Dose Project.[1] We, as readers, extracted information from pharmaceutical periodicals on drug-drug interaction, side effects and dosages. With the stroke of a computer key, nurses and doctors accessed information on drugs: an early form of Google. In the sixties, when the mainframe was six stories high, this was an exciting innovation for safely mixing medicines.

In the twenty-first century global community, our medical choices multiplied far beyond most wild dreamers. David

Eisenberg, as an MD based at Harvard, gathered "alternative health care" data eventually published in 1993.[2] At the time–1990–money being spent on alternative health care defined massage and fifteen other categories including yoga, prayer and biofeedback. The results rocked the medical field to its financial underpinnings. The bottom line: more than $13 billion was spent by consumers in the United States for alternative health care. Ten billion of that was spent out of pocket.

More and more, we Americans mix our remedies, our conventional and alternative healing practices. Of course, we need to do this wisely.

Integrating Our Healing Practices. I like working with physicians who go to acupuncturists, massage therapists, yoga or tai chi/chi kung/aikido classes. If you cannot find an MD or DO with this type of openness to alternatives, try to find out if your doctor's life partner visits such alternative health care practitioners. Likewise, the best alternative health care practitioners are generous in their openness to whatever heal, maintaining good working relationships with MDs, DOs,

---

Golden Rule

BAHAI
If you seek justice, choose for others what you would choose for yourself. - The Bayan

BRAHMANISM
Never do unto other what would hurt you if done unto you. –Mahabharata 5:15

BUDDHISM
Do not offend others as you would not like to be offended. –Udanavarga 5:18

CHRISTIANITY
Do unto others as you would like them to do unto you. –Matt. 7:12

chiropractors, naturopaths, acupuncturists and other licensed and respected health care professionals.

First Do No Harm. Witches and the medical doctors use the same principle: *primum no nocere* ("First do no harm"). This should be the foundation for all our actions. When and how shall we use the plethora of healing options available to us?

In the late sixties at the University of Iowa, the anthropologist Margaret Mead told a story from her daughter Mary Catherine Bateson's childhood. Walking with a slightly older friend to a neighbor's home, halfway there, Mary Catherine was bitten by a bug or got a sliver. Her friend asked which direction she wanted to go for medical help, back to her father or forward to the friend's home? Mary Catherine's replied that if she needed help with a thinking problem, she would go back to her father at home. But as she needed help with a wound, she would go forward to the neighbor who was much better at doctoring.[3]

What a delightful example of consciousness and discernment. Mary Catherine's decision was based on choosing the best way to meet her needs.

CONFUCIANISM
What we do not wish to be done to us, let us not do it to others. –Analects 15:23

HINDUISM
This is the sum of duty: do not do to others what would cause pain if done to you. –Mahabhat 5:817

ISLAM
No one will be a true believer unless he wished for others what he wishes for himself. –Sunnatt

JAINISM
One should treat all creatures in the world as one would like to be treated. –Mahabharata

JUDAISM
What you do not wish for yourself, do not wish for others. –Talmud Shabbat 31:A

Remove the insult, pacify, restore and integrate.
This fundamental principle of medical treatment is also a trusty
guide for your own health.

Remove the Insult. A sliver in the hand is straightfor-
ward: remove the splinter, remove the insult. Yet the insult isn't
always clear. Sometimes it takes scrutiny to identify the insult.
For example, if half of us cough and sneeze after we enjoy imi-
tation ice cream made with fake fat and high-fructose corn syrup, it's time to realize that extremely cold food and drink and
corn syrup are insults to remove from our diets.

What other habits insult our health and beauty?

Painful knees and shortness of breath are reactions some
people have to iced foods and drinks or to foods containing
corn syrup. Dry skin can be a symptom of too little good fat
in the diet. Disturbed sleep might be the paradoxical result of
napping in the afternoon. When you have a complaint, remove
a little of the insult. Read the labels on your food purchases.
Do not eat high-fructose corn syrup. Stop with the iced drinks.
As your awareness grows, your sensitivity to insults becomes

MASONRY
*Be with your friend the same way you are with your-
self. -Old Script*

MAYA SCIENCE
You are myself. We are all one. -Popol Vuh

MOHAWK
*If my warriors are to fight, there are too few. If they are
to die, there are too many.*

MOTHER KNOWLEDGE
Be kind. Be gentle. –Ancient Ethics

NATIVE SPIRITUALITY
*We are as much alive as we keep the earth alive. -Chief
Dan George*

PAGAN
Harm none. -Most Ancient Law

more sophisticated. Listening to your intuition humming in your tummy often translates into remembered body brilliance.

Pacify. When we pacify, we bring ourselves into a state of calm, peace, quiet, and rest. Sleep, the wet nurse of all healing, begins to rescue us from trauma. Sleep is still a biological mystery. No matter how much it has been studied, scientists still don't know exactly what sleep is, but many traditions have something to say about sleep. For instance, Ayurvedic teachings say that dreaming of running, flying or swimming means the nervous system is happily balancing. Years ago, I read about Russian doctors treating psychotic breaks with thirty days of sleep! I have never talked with anyone who experienced thirty days of sleep, but I know how much I like a good night's sleep. "A good night's sleep is worth a million dollars," my elders would say over morning coffee.

Resting is often difficult for Americans. We are addicted to action. We are human "beings" not human "doings." Usually, there is no one outside holding a gun to our heads to consume,

---

PAIUTE
Pray for others, not yourself. If we all do this we, each, will have all we need.

SIKHISM
I am a stranger to no one; and no one is a stranger to me. Indeed, I am a friend to all. -Guru Granter Sahib

TAOISM
Make as yours the profits of your fellowman as well as his loss. -T'ai-Shang Kin-Ying P'ien

UNITARIANISM
We affirm and promote respect for the interdependent web of all existence of which we are all a part. -Unitarian principle

ZORASTRIANISM
Do not do unto others whatever is injurious to yourself. - Shayazi.ni.Shayast 13.29

consume, consume more media, food, products, activities—consume the concept of consumption. More than thirty percent of the US population experiences difficulty falling asleep or awakens in the middle of the night with a mind full of loud details. In Africa, waking in the middle of night often means one is starving. Here in the United States, it often means one is experiencing a problem with overconsumption: inappropriate quantity, quality, time or temperature. A surprisingly large proportion of clients complain of waking in the middle of the night, often with indigestion. Consistently, they eat late in the evening, which almost always contributes to sleep problems.

Besides eating appropriate amounts (that which would fill the space made by bringing your right hand and left hand together to make a bowl) at appropriate times (no later than 5 p.m. if you are older than fifty five), touch and movement are major sources of pacification. Try holding your hands as in prayer and placing them over your heart: observe your breath and focus on your comfort level. Or place your hands on either side of your face, cupping your cheeks with your palms. Hold your face as if you were your own grandmother, getting ready to plant a kiss. Do you feel cradled and appreciated? Lace your fingers behind your head, holding them where your neck meets your skull. Move your elbows closer together and then farther apart. Does this make you feel enfolded and supported, reassured? We can nurture ourselves and others with simple, pacifying touches like these.

Restore. When we restore we bring back to a state of health, vigor and soundness. Restorative interventions include all forms of rest: the refreshing quiet or repose of sleep; ease or inactivity after exertion; relief from anything that wearies, troubles or disturbs. Restoration can come from enjoying a period of supported inactivity; tranquility; mental and spiritual calm such as meditation, restorative yoga, acupuncture or a long, deeply relaxing massage. You choose among these great healers, following your sense of what's needed whenever you seek to restore your beauty, health and sense of well-being.

For deep rest, consider a class in restorative yoga. After class, you will feel as if you had taken a trip to an internal land of luxurious living. Dollars to donuts, your sleep will be creamy and dreamy after a four-hour restorative class. Caveat: do not mess with caffeine, other drugs, rich foods or violent movies after class. Judith Lasater's restorative yoga book, *Relax and Renew* is a step-by-step description of poses to calm and pacify every place in your body and soul.[4]

A couple of years ago, at the local community college, I taught yoga to the baseball team. The team was crazy for Savasana, the corpse pose. In Savasana, the last pose we did, often one or two of them would fall asleep and snore. When I saw them on campus, they chanted "yoga, yoga, yoga" and then "Savasana, Savasana, Savasana" to the rhythm of sis-boom-bah—true cheerleaders!

The most important part of any yoga practice: ending in the corpse pose, lying on your back, knees flat or slightly elevated by a small blanket roll, legs separated eight to ten inches. With my team, I walked around the room adjusting hands, necks, shoulders and feet, pulling, placing, aligning forms as they settled with gravity. Tucked under a blanket, one generally moves into a state of deep relaxation. We need to do this every day: tucked under, in deep relaxation. This particular tool is the seatbelt for the next four score.

Integrate. Integration brings together and incorporates the whole; to integrate is to unify. Beauty is born and health abides when healthy cells support optimal function of the microcosm and the macrocosm.

With my baseball team, I see rest allowing integration of "doing" —the doing of the day and life as well as the doing of asanas, postures. Lying still in Savasana restores. Savasana also allows them to integrate what they have learned from moving during our session. Integrative practice should be part of all sports: restore, and in the process, integrate.

The guidelines for mixing elements in health care follow rainbow reality. In my northern California springtime sky, it is impossible to find the precise line in a rainbow where red stops and orange begins. There is clearly defined red and clearly defined orange, but some of the breathtaking beauty of the rainbow is the merging of red and orange, the mixing space, the meeting space. Healing and health care practices blend as rainbows blend. Each of the four healing steps merge with what has gone before and what follows. Removing the insult merges with pacifying, pacifying merges with restoration. Restoration merges with integration just as red merges with orange merges with yellow and so on to violet.

Let me offer an example from my own life. As I write this, the local authorities have issued pollen warnings. Spring falls from the trees, yellow casings hang gliding off oaks, pine dust drifting in the wind. We've had days of yellow blizzards, the worst in years, as summer hits hard and fast. I sneeze so many times, my Spanish-speaking friend wishes me in turn health, wealth, love—salud, dinero, amor—then long life, running out of blessings as the repetitive sneezing continues. Like every injury or affliction, "hay fevering" teaches me. The symptoms—sneezing, itching, coughing, swelling face, fever and headache—appear to be time-limited to six weeks and escapable if I change locations. But appearance is not reality, the universe laughs. I visit Philadelphia to get out of northern California and find the East Coast pollen count has set a record high. (Nevertheless, hay fevering has given me the incentive to travel in springtime, and by now my travels have taken me all over the world.)

I am continually coached on how to remove the insult. I stay inside during the springtime afternoon high winds. I find or make safer environments. I walk at the reservoir where—even though we are thirty miles from the coast—clean ocean air makes its way through valleys, sweetening each breath. Using a HEPA air filter in my bedroom creates an inside island, a free zone. I ask for and receive support: prayers, cookies made with spelt flour rather than wheat flour to avoid possible "sensitivities" or allergies, food without corn syrup or high-fructose, prescription drugs and sprays from my dear medical doctors. Sipping more than a gallon a day of spring or distilled water helps keep the mucus clear.

My Goal: to be healthy and educated about allergies and sensitivities. Therefore, my task is to uncover the relationships between the natural world and my behavior during springtime pollination. I do this with moderate exercise, restful sleep and responsible work while choosing correct foods, food concentrates, supplements, and medications. Meanwhile, I continue meditation and acupuncture as well as practices outlined in this book, such as foot massage and oiling. They calm my nervous system, soothe my irritated mucosa and generally restore my sense of well-being.

In my tub of clean dechlorinated water, washing helps remove insults by rinsing pollen from my body as it pacifies and restores my spirit. While I soak, I also irrigate my nostrils with saline solution in a neti pot. The neti pot comes from India, part of the Ayurvedic and Siddha Vaidya tradition. Looking just like a little teapot, it holds eight ounces of warm saline solution, the right amount to irrigate one nostril. As the bath washes insults from my skin and hair, the neti pot cleans my

nasal passages. This is NOT a good practice if "green goop" has taken up residence in your nostrils. See your MD, DO, Naturopathic doctor, chiropracter or other health care practitioner for immediate treatment. Green is not a color you want coming out of your nose.

Here's what you need for nasal irrigation: A neti pot or a twenty-four ounce bottle with pop-up lid, spring water and noniodized salt. I use salt from the Grand Canyon harvested by Native Americans, Celtic salt or other health food salt without iodine. My preference is for clean, additive-free, earthbound salts. To make a saline solution appropriate for nose, throat and eye wash, mix a heaping 1/4 teaspoon of finely ground noniodized salt (table salt) or a slightly rounded 1/2 teaspoon of coarsely ground salt (kosher salt) in the pot or bottle with eight ounces of clean warm water (spring, distilled or filtered water without chemical contaminates). Swirl or stir until the salt is completely dissolved.

The temperature of the water is important. Too cold will give you a headache and too hot will burn your nose. Your external skin temperature is 93 degrees Fahrenheit. Although body temperature inside the mouth varies, 98.6 degrees is typical. The water should be tepid: if it's comfortable for your wrist, using the same temperature gauge as to judge a baby's bottle, it will be perfect for your nose.

If your nostrils are clogged: for five minutes pat your face with a hot, damp towel (heated in the microwave) to open up your sinuses or steam your face over a saucepan of boiled water. Turn off the stove. Use a towel to make a tent. I use an electric rice cooker, uncovered, with three cups of simmering water.

To use the neti pot, hold it in one hand, and leaning forward over a sink, tilt your head to one side and pour the contents gently through the upper nostril. The water will run out the other nostril. Stand up and wipe your nose. Repeat on the other side. The thinking these days is that "sniffing" in and then spitting is better than blowing your nose. If you blow your nose to clear the nostril, open your mouth first and blow very gently. You can drive infection deep into your head if you blow too hard. Do not take that risk. Do not force anything.

When I'm on the road, I carry my salt in a film canister, tight and dry. I use a twenty-four-ounce "sportpack" spring water bottle with a pop-up lid for nasal irrigation, making a perfect recyclable neti pot. I add salt to the bottle and shake well; then the bottle takes a hot bath with me. Five or ten minutes brings the salt water to tepid, the perfect temperature for delicate nasal tissues.

To restore my health from the draining effects of hay fever, I examine my habits. These ingrained responses either support or destroy health and beauty. A change in one tiny habit and the world changes dramatically. We see in the macrocosm how small things make a huge difference: as they say, the flutter of a butterfly's wings in one hemisphere shows up as a storm in the other hemisphere, affecting global weather. In the microcosm, we see this at work on our sleep. One tiny change—a walk around the block, herbal tea instead of black tea, a steaming, or a rinse with the neti pot, and sleep is restored!

To increase the restorative impact of my own sleep, I follow what our great-grandparents practiced. It is working for me. Try it yourself: finish eating solid foods by 5 p.m., giving your body time to produce melatonin, the hormone of deep sleep. Go to sleep by 10 p.m., get up by 6 a.m. Avoid cold drinks and napping during the day. Listen to soothing music and smell fragrant aromas in the evening. If you stick by your ancestral wisdom, you are likely to find, as I have, that two-thirds of the sleep difficulties reduce dramatically or disappear. Half of the remaining insomnia might diminish with regular massage, acupuncture, yoga or meditation. The remainder will disappear when you turn off the television and computer in the evening. Try it out. As my mother said to my grandfather when he didn't want a foot massage all those years ago. "Try it, Dad. You'll like it." Experiment with these pacifying, restorative practices by doing one or two of them gently and regularly for forty consecutive days. Mark it on your calendar. If you skip a day or two, start again.

Every day, we are offered opportunities to learn and improve our lives. In my tale of hay fevering, removing the insult, pacifying and restoring have had an integrative effect. As I write this, after several years of integrating ancient and innovative healing traditions and techniques, I am healthy enough to enjoy spring at home in gorgeous Northern California.

❀ ❀ ❀

Notes

1 Unit Dose Project, University of Iowa, Iowa City, Iowa. Unit-dose dispensing of medication was developed in the 1960s to support nurses in medication administration and reduce the waste of increasingly expensive medications. Most of the investigations of medication errors and unit-dose dispensing took place from 1970 to 1976. Now, unit-dose dispensing of medications is a standard of practice at hospitals in the United States. www.ahrq.gov

2 David M. Eisenberg, MD, et al., "Unconventional Medicine in the United States: Prevalence, Costs, and Patterns of Use," *New England Journal of Medicine* 328, January 28, 1993, pp. 246-252.

3 Margaret Mead, PhD, University of Iowa Guest Lecture Series, Iowa City, IA: circa 1970.

4 Judith Lasater, PT, PhD, *Relax and Renew*, Berkeley, CA: Rodmell Press, 1995.

8

Conclusion

In the introduction, I invited you to accompany me on a journey of healing. Now, even though this book is coming to an end, I must tell you that the journey is not. In my life as in yours, each discovery leads to new opportunities and in turn to new discoveries. In the most recent stage of the journey, my "hay fevering" has led me halfway around the world.

As I wrote in the last chapter, for twelve springs hay fever defined the season. At first I figured I could tough it out like all my fellow sufferers, but sneezing and swelling got progressively worse. Allopathic prescriptions barely touched the symptoms. Over-the-counter pills worked best, but still had uncomfortable side effects. After two miserable springtimes, I packed my bags. For eight years, I traveled during the hay fevering season. While I regretted missing the wonderful weather at home, I traded it for adventure: China, Europe, the Grand Canyon, making lemons into refreshing lemonade. I studied health care, worked and traveled without a trace of "fevering" even in heavily polluted Beijing.

But my goal was health, not a life designed to avoiding certain seasons. I wanted to enjoy spring at home. So after returning from each trip, I invested in a new, intensive "alternative" treatment, sometimes several: weekly acupuncture, ten-day courses of colonics, ten-day silent vipassana meditations, curious diets, homeopathic remedies, food concentrates and supplements. Culling what worked from this research, I put together a doable program, a healing practice I could afford.

Even though I was a student of the healing arts, I still relied on over-the-counter antihistamines, and aspirin with lots of downtime recovering from raging battles in my sinuses. The skirmishes became less violent, but they exhausted me. Having to cancel appointments with clients and spending several days sleeping off the ravages of internal storms kept me searching for solutions.

In the spring of 2003, a new path opened on my journey. As the walnut trees eased up on their reproductive orgy and my hypersensitive tissues began to trust the world again, a friend called to invite me to a gathering. The attractions were Sunday evening dessert and a lecture on ancient medical practices by an orthopedic physician. As I am a pushover for her desserts and had Sunday night open, I concluded it was meant to be.

The beautiful and brilliant South Indian doctor began by defining a term entirely new to me: Siddha Vaidya, subatomic medicine practiced in the Dravidian culture thousands of years before the Ayurvedic tradition came into being in northern India.

He told us that the matriarchal Dravidians were contemporary with the Mesopotamians and ancient Egyptians. They identified 4,448 diseases and thirty-two internal and thirty-two external specific remedies for each of these diseases. Mixing these ingredients produced hundreds of thousands of possible combinations capable of treating disorders. Among the thousands of diseases these ancients identified were autoimmune disorders, seven types of malaria, nine fetal disorders which could be treated in utero as well as a number of medical conditions I have witnessed but cannot name because they could not be identified by contemporary allopathic practitioners. Archeologists date these discoveries seven to nine thousand years in the past; our lecturer that evening estimated that they had originated fourteen thousand years ago.

As I listened, two questions came to mind. I posed a neurological question which the doctor answered simply and clearly. Then I asked a geographic question: how close is this clinic to snorkeling?

He laughed.

Giving myself incentives to finish this book, I had promised myself that after the manuscript was shepherded into the world, I could go offshore to study neurology and physiology somewhere I could snorkel.

His answer: forty-five minutes by air from the clinic are the Maldives, home to some of the best snorkeling in the world.

The good doctor described a technique called kaya hot oil massage. Medicated oil is heated to between 180 and 270 degrees Fahrenheit. Homemade muslin pouches containing common herbs are heated in an electric pot in 1/6 inch of medicated oil. After a lubricating massage of warm medicated oil to get the body saturated and ready for smooth application, the heated, oily pouches are rapidly drawn over the body. The skilled practitioner's movements are so quick that there is no damage to the skin, only a pleasant sensation of warmth.

The kaya hot oil treatment is administered in a course. Consecutive days of treatment are followed by an equal number of days of complete rest. Three-, five- or seven-day treatments result in a combined treatment and rest period of six, ten or fourteen days. No one is to receive more than fourteen days a year of this treatment, for a total of no more than seven years.

Other treatment constraints are simple and soothing: no news, no scary stories, no work. For entertainment, silly stories generating pheromones are most conducive to healing. Under treatment, clients eat nutritiously, avoiding certain foods that are believed to contradict the treatment, sleep early and avoid stressful situations.

How does it work? The good doctor explained that bodily regeneration and degeneration are considered byproducts of two main cellular processes: growth (anabolic) and decay (catabolic). Bringing these two processes into equilibrium supports an optimal cellular metabolic state. Encoded in our DNA is the potential for long life: balanced regeneration and degeneration for a hundred years, maybe more. Like almost all health care practitioners, I believe it is possible to recover balance and reestablish order in the human system. Perhaps kaya hot oil massage and other treatments and medicines available from Siddha Vaidya physicians were capable of reversing disorders such as sinusitis. I felt this was the next step in my healing quest. I signed up to learn the treatment protocol.

I observed the simple, elegant secret of the kaya treatment. High heat applied without harm encourages the body to release hormones, neuropeptides and other healing substances and energies, healing you from the inside out. The treatment feels

good, like being in the sun. You are healed by relaxing, resting, being drenched in warm oil, scrubbing clean and sleeping. You are healed by your own miracle of existence!

Traditionally, kaya hot oil treatments were used to rejuvenate and extend the lives of royalty and holy sages. Siddha Vaidya was repressed by colonizers in India, Sri Lanka and Singapore, yet the tradition was handed down through the generations to show up in my northern California valley. It's hard to think of any other healing practice I have enjoyed more, either as giver or receiver.

Every time I start a kaya hot oil series for a client, I bless this tradition and my good fortune in knowing a little Siddha Vaidya. Every time I am up to my elbows in the medicated oil, skin glistening on my client's body as on my own arms, I say a prayer of thanks.

This is powerful healing. I see changes happen each day of the treatment. Over the several days of treatment, when a client lies face down on the table, the space between the ankle and the table gets smaller and smaller as ligaments elongate. In old and young alike, the stiff and cramped body lengthen. Spastic paraplegics relax. The overweight lose pounds and regain full use of joints. Life is full of small miracles. You and I see them, sometimes more, sometimes less frequently. But with these hot oil treatments, miracles constantly unfold.

As I've written elsewhere, the biggest obstacle to healing is often people's reluctance to make the small sacrifices or investments needed to change harmful habits or mobilize healing energies. I've written in these pages about individuals who were unwilling to give up milk or other foods that make their lives a misery, for instance.

With respect to kaya hot oil treatment, the obstacle is time. For many Americans, the thought of devoting a full week or even two to absolute rest is almost impossible to conceive. *Doing* overrides *being* even when we are offered the opportunity to regenerate and reverse the aging process. Why sacrifice healing for a few more days of busyness?

Calling Myself a Healer. There's no telling where my study of Siddha Vaidya will take me. I only know I want to continue the journey as long as possible, meeting all the challenges it throws in my path. Now, after writing enthusiastically about the importance of calling things by their right names, I have been challenged to identify myself.

As I said in the introduction, I am a student of healing and a doctor of what works. For years I have been unwilling to call myself a healer. It sounds presumptuous. Generally, when I am introduced as a healer, the first item of business after thanking my hosts is to clarify the fact that I am a student of the art and science of healing and health care traditions. I've been comfortable in this role.

But recently, my comfort was confronted by another shaman, the biggest man I have ever met, surprisingly dressed in a smartly fashioned gold, yellow and orange camouflage kilt. Looking like a version of Neptune with his trident, he demonstrated his healing instrument, a giant tuning fork.

"Tell me if anything is too much," the shaman said. The feeling was extraordinary. Vibrations coursed through my belly, heat rose in my lower back, oscillating my umbilicus and navel sphincter muscle. Tuning, I received a tune-up. Organs lifted. It felt good, both gentle and powerful.

The ten-minute demonstration complete, we chatted briefly about divine light rays and sacred sounds. Then the shaman gave me a message: "Between November 7th and November 13th, you must begin calling yourself a healer."

My eyebrows went up.

"You are one," he continued. "It is important for your work to call yourself a healer. It is important for you to recognize your power."

"Okay," I said, "how about this? I am willing to call myself a 'student in training to be a healer.'"

"By November 13th," he replied, "everyone will recognize that you are a healer, even you."

As I contemplate calling myself a healer, I realize it isn't so presumptuous after all. I know I can touch you, and usually you will feel better as a result. Remember the man I told you about in the introduction, who asked his doctor if massage would help? The doctor replied, "No, it will just feel good." Feeling good is healing. I can be a healer and so can you.

Once again, I am being challenged to take some of my own medicine. We can do this, you and I. If I can write down what I know, presenting my gifts to you, if I can call myself a healer—if I can do what I once felt to be beyond my wildest dreams—you too can deliver your gifts to the world. We can do this together, one step at a time.

I've often thought that one's life, if you look at it, is rather like the night sky. Suddenly you see a star whose light has never been visible before. Not because it hadn't been there but because the light took so long to reach you. The light is the meaning; light is not only the light.

Childhood is full of stars whose light only reaches one now. Suddenly you look at the very familiar night sky and you say, "My God, there's another one there." It's been there ever since the beginning but you didn't see it. You didn't see the meaning of it.

Sir Laurens van der Post appearing in *Hasten Slowly*, a film by Micke Lemle.

—a young Denali

Amen. Ah women!

APPENDIX

Language of Western Anatomy and Movement

By convention and in agreement with the International Committee on Anatomical Nomenclature, we agree to certain terms when we describe the human body in space.

In humans, portions of the body which are closer to the head end are "superior" (Latin meaning upper); those which are farther away are "inferior" (Latin meaning lower). "Superior" corresponds to cranial, at the skull, or cephalic, at the head and "inferior" corresponds to caudal, at the tail. Objects near the front are "anterior"; those near the rear are "posterior." Anterior corresponds to the term "ventral", forward surface, and "dorsal" corresponds to rear surface.

Terms of Motion

By agreement, the standard anatomical position in humans is standing upright, facing forward, feet directly placed under the ishium or " sit bones," arms hanging at the sides and palms facing forward.

Anatomical terms of motion refer to changes away from the standard anatomical position. When the human body is lying down, this position becomes supine, with the palms facing up. Supine, Latin for going backward or lying on the back, describes the body and hands. When the arms rotate and palm faces posteriorly (or downwards when seated), the description of the body is still "supine" but the arms and hands are in the prone position, facing downward. We describe the movement of turning the hand from prone to supine as supination; turning the hand from supine to prone is pronation. Pronation results in crossing of the radius (bone) with respect to the ulna.

Relative Directions

Structures near the midline are called medial and those near the sides are called lateral. For example, your cheeks are lateral to your nose and the tip of the nose is in the median line. Ipsilateral means on the same side, contralateral means on the other side and bilateral means on both sides.

Sagittal, Latin "like an arrow," refers to the spine dividing the body into right and left equal halves. Therefore, medial structures are closer to the midsagittal plane, lateral structures are farther from the midsagittal plane.

Specialized terms are used to describe location on appendages, parts that have a point of attachment to the main trunk of the body. Structures closer to the point of attachment of the body are proximal or central, while ones more distant from the attachment point are distal or peripheral. For example, the hands are at the distal end of the arms, while the shoulders are at the proximal ends.

These terms can also be used in relationship to organs, such as the proximal end of the urethra is attached to the bladder.

Objects and surfaces closer to or facing towards the head are cranial; those facing away or farther from the head are caudal.

Structures on or closer to the body's surface are superficial (or external) and those farther inside are profound or deep (or internal).

When speaking of inner organs, visceral means attached to or associated with an organ, while parietal refers to a structure associated with or attached to the body wall (the chest wall or the abdominal wall). For example, pleura is a single structure, for convenience the term "visceral pleura" refers to that part attached to the outer surface of the lung, and "parietal pleura" refers to that part attached to the inside of the chest wall.

The sides of the forearm are named after its bones: Structures closer to the radius are radial, structures closer to the ulna are ulnar, and structures relating to both bones are referred to as radioulnar. Similarly, in the lower leg, structures near the tibia (shinbone) are tibial and structures near the fibula are fibular (or peroneal).

Movement in the body

Flexion—Bending movement which decreases the angle between two parts. Bending the elbow, or clenching a hand into a fist, are examples of flexion. When sitting down, the knees are flexed. Flexion of the hip or shoulder moves the limb forward or towards the anterior side of the body.

Extension—The opposite of flexion; a straightening movement that increases the angle between body parts. In a yoga four-point, "on all fours", the fingers are fully extended. When standing, the knees are extended. Extension of the hip or shoulder moves the limb backward or towards the posterior side of the body.

Hyperextension—Movement of a body part beyond the normal range of motion, such as the position of the head when looking upwards into the heavens or "locking knees."

Movement in relation to midline of body

Abduction—Motion that pulls a structure away from the midline of the body or, in the case of fingers and toes, spreading the digits apart, away from the centerline of the hand or foot. Raising the arms laterally, to the sides, is an example of abduction.

Adduction—Motion that pulls a structure towards the midline of the body, or towards the midline of a limb. Hugging the arms to the chest or bringing the knees together, are examples of adduction. In the case of the fingers or toes, adduction is closing the digits together.

Movement up and down

Elevation—Movement in a superior direction. This term is often applied to the shoulders as in shrugging shoulders.

Depression—Movement in an inferior direction, the opposite of elevation. One shoulder is depressed, the other is elevated.

Movement of the foot & Movement of the toes

Dorsiflexion—Flexion of the entire foot superiorly, or upwards towards the nose. Dorsiflexion in yoga asanas provide protection for the vulnerable knees. Dorsiflex just your toes.

Plantarflexion—Flexion of the entire foot inferiorly, or downwards as when one extends her toes like a ballerina on point. Plantarflex just your foot! Plantarflex just your toes!

Movement of the sole of the foot

Eversion—The movement of the sole of the foot away from the median plane or out to the side, knees by default move toward the midline.

Inversion—The movement of the sole towards the median plane as if you were putting the soles of your feet together in prayer.

There are additional descriptions of the anatomical body in motion but the information presented here is a substantial beginning to the accepted language of body movement.

GLOSSARY

Most references are taken from the world wide web. To the best of the author's knowledge, information is accurate and truthful. However, the author appreciates comments and corrections. If there are additional entries the reader desires, please submit requests and suggestions to darca@darcaleenicholson.com

Alexander Technique—F. Matthias Alexander(1869–1955) was an Australian actor and teacher. He originally developed the Alexander Technique as a method of vocal training for singers and actors in the 1890s. While Alexander was developing his method of voice training, he realized that the basis for all successful vocal education was an efficiently and naturally functioning respiratory mechanism. So, in teaching voice, Alexander focused primarily on helping the breathing mechanism to function more effectively. Because of his focus on "reeducating" the breathing mechanism, some of Alexander's students, who had come to him for vocal training, found that their respiratory difficulties also improved. These improvements were recognized by medical doctors who began referring their patients with respiratory ailments to Alexander for help. In this way, F.M. Alexander's technique of vocal training developed into a technique he termed "respiratory reeducation."

Alexander also discovered that habitual breathing and vocal patterns are parts of habitual patterns of general coordination. In fact, many problems we see as involving just one particular part of the body, e.g. lower back pain and "RSI," (Repetitive Strain Injury) are often symptoms of larger habitual patterns of malcoordination.

Alexander regarded the empirical scientific method to be the foundation of his work. He used self-observation and reasoning to make effortless the physical acts of everyday movement: sitting, standing, walking, using the hands and speaking. He designed his methods to make experimentation and training deliberately repeatable, and to learn in a way that would allow continuing improvement from any starting point.

The Alexander Technique educates the student's sense of kinesthesia or proprioception. This sense is used to calibrate internally one's own bodily location and weight and to judge the effort necessary for moving. The Alexander Technique also educates how to carry intent more fully into action with reasoning and constructive thinking techniques.

According to Alexander teachers, few adults in Western culture retain their ability to move freely without needless self-imposed interference. Given an unceasing cumulative demand that unnecessarily stresses the body's structural design, the price as adults grow older can range from feelings of stress and resignation to very real physical problems, due to movement limitations that could be changed.
www.alexandertechnique.com

Alimentary Canal—Also called the digestive tract, the alimentary canal is the pathway by which food enters the body and solid wastes are expelled. The alimentary canal includes the mouth, pharynx, esophagus, stomach, small intestine, large intestine, and anus. Actions include: mastication or chewing, swallowing, digestion, absorption, recycling and elimination of waste materials.

Allopathic Medicine—The term was coined by Samuel Hahnemann to differentiate homeopathic practices from conventional medicine, based on the types of treatments used. The term *allopath* comes from the Greek roots meaning "opposite" and "disease."

As used by homeopaths, the term "allopathy" has always referred to a principle of curing disease by administering substances that produce the opposite effect of the disease when given to a healthy human. Hahnemann used this term to distinguish medicine as practiced in his time from his use of minute doses of substances to treat the spiritual causes of illness.

Allopathic Medicine is used by Association of American Medical Colleges, American Medical Association and Accreditation Council for Graduate Medical Education to denote a name for orthodox medicine when necessary to distinguish it from other medicinal paradigms.
www.medterms.com

Asana—Western meaning: yoga posture or pose. Sanskrit literal translation: sitting posture, seat. Immobile bodily posture a person assumes in order to isolate the mind. The third of eight prescribed stages designed to lead the aspirant to samadhi, the state of utterly profound contemplation of The Absolute.

Ayurvedic Medicine—or Ayurveda, meaning Life Knowledge, or Science of Life defines guidelines for healthy daily living, a way of life designed around energetic concepts and relationships of Pitta (fire and earth), Vata (air and ether) and Kapha (earth and water) in Tridosha, the internal balance between the elements.

Borborygmus—(plural borborygmi) from Greek is the rumbling sound produced by the movement of gas through the intestines of animals. The "rumble" sometimes heard from the stomach is a normal part of digestion. Rumbles may also occur when there is incomplete digestion of food leading to excess gas in the intestine as well as when there is a "relaxation reflex."

Bowen Technique or Therapy—versions of a group of technical interpretations of the work of Australian self-proclaimed osteopath Tom Bowen (1916–1982).

The Bowen Technique was limited to Australia until 1986, four years after Bowen's death. It has since been developed and furthered by many others. For example: Dr. Kevin Ryan teaches his interpretation of the Bowen Technique to Osteopathic students at the Royal Melbourne Institute of Technology. www.bowentherapytechnique.com

Cisplatin—cis-diamminedichloroplatinum (II) (CDDP) is a platinum-based chemotherapy drug used to treat various types of cancers, including sarcomas, some carcinomas (e.g. small cell lung cancer and ovarian cancer), lymphomas and germ cell tumors. It was the first member of its class, which now also includes carboplatin and oxaliplatin.

Conjugated Linoleic Acid (CLA)—is a good fat that may be a potent cancer fighter. In animal studies, very small amounts of CLA have blocked all three stages of cancer: 1) initiation, 2) promotion, and 3) metastasis. Most anti-cancer agents block only one of these stages. CLA has been shown to slow the growth of an unusually wide variety of tumors, including cancers of the skin, breast, prostate, and colon.

On the molecular level, CLA resembles another type of fat called "linoleic acid" or LA. (Both CLA and LA have 18 carbon atoms and two double bonds holding the chain together. The main difference is in the placement of those bonds.) However, CLA and LA appear to have opposite effects on the human body. For example, LA promotes tumor growth but CLA blocks it.

A recent survey determined that women with the most CLA in their diets had a 60 percent reduction in the risk of breast cancer.

CLA found in nature does not have any known negative side effects. The most abundant source of natural CLA is the meat and dairy products of grass fed animals. Research conducted since 1999 shows that grazing animals have from 3–5 times more CLA than animals fattened on grain in a feedlot. Switching from grain fed to grass fed products appears to greatly increase your intake of CLA.
www.eatwild.com

Connective Tissue—one of the four types of tissue in traditional classifications (the others being epithelial, muscle, and nervous tissue.) It is largely a category of exclusion rather than one with a precise definition, but all or most tissues in this category are similarly:

* Involved in structure and support.

* Derived from mesoderm (there are exceptions).

* Characterized largely by traits of nonliving tissue.

Blood, cartilage, and bone are usually considered connective tissue, but because they differ so substantially from the other tissues in this class, the phrase "connective tissue proper" is commonly used to exclude those three. There is also variation in the classification of embryonic connective tissues; in this notation they will be treated as a third and separate category.

Connective tissue proper

* Dense connective tissue (or, less commonly, fibrous connective tissue) forms ligaments and tendons. Its densely packed collagen fibers have great tensile strength.
* Areolar (or loose) connective tissue holds organs and epithelia in place, and has a variety of proteinaceous fibers, including collagen and elastin. It is also important in inflammation.
* Reticular connective tissue is a network of reticular fibers (fine collagen) that form a soft skeleton to support the lymphoid organs (lymph nodes, bone marrow, and spleen.)
* Adipose tissue contains adipocytes, used for cushioning, insulation, lubrication (primarily in the pericardium) and energy storage or fat.

Specialized connective tissues

* Blood functions in transport. Its extracellular matrix is blood plasma, which transports dissolved nutrients, hormones, and carbon dioxide in the form of bicarbonate. The main cellular component is red blood cells.
* Cartilage. In most vertebrates, cartilage is found primarily in joints, where it provides cushioning. The extracellular matrix of cartilage is composed primarily of collagen.
* Bone makes up virtually the entire skeleton in adult vertebrates.

Embryonic connective tissues

* Mesenchymal connective tissue
* Mucous connective tissue

Embryo—from Greek *embryon* meaning a young one. In humans, the developing organism from conception until approximately the end of the second month. Embryological, embryonic.

Feldenkrais Movement Method—Moshé Pinhas Feldenkrais, DS, (1904–1984) founded the Feldenkrais method after a knee injury and considerable research.

"There is little doubt in my mind that the motor function, and perhaps the muscles themselves, are part and parcel of our higher functions. This is not true only of those higher functions like singing, painting and loving, which are impossible without muscular activity, but also of thinking, recalling, remembering and feeling.

The advantage of approaching the unity of mental and muscular life through the body lies in the fact that the muscle expression is simpler because it is concrete and easier to locate. It is also incomparably easier to make a person aware of what is happening in the body, therefore the body approach yields faster and more direct results. On acting on the significant parts of the body, such as the eyes, the neck, the breath, or the pelvis, it is easy to effect striking changes of mood on the spot."

The Method, designed to improve human functioning by exploring the relationship between movement and consciousness, integrates Ju Jits, other somatic approaches, human engineering, evolution and psychology.

Dr. Feldenkrais authored numerous books on learning, human consciousness and somatic experience as well as created thousands of movement and method lessons.

The extent and breath of his collaborative influence in the world of consciousness and integrative healing movement cannot be overestimated.
www.feldenkrais-method.org

Genetically Modified Organisms, Genetically Altered Material—GMO is an organism whose genetic

material has been altered using genetic engineering techniques generally known as recombinant DNA technology. Recombinant DNA technology is the ability to combine DNA molecules from different sources (i.e., rat genes into salmon eggs, or across species) into one molecule in a test tube. Thus, the abilities or the phenotype of the organism, or the proteins it produces, can be altered through the modification of its genes.

GM Products: Benefits and Controversies

Benefits (Who pays for the evaluation?)

* Crops
    o Enhanced taste and quality
    o Reduced maturation time
    o Increased nutrients, yields, and stress tolerance
    o Improved resistance to disease, pests, and herbicides
    o New products and growing techniques

* Animals
    o Increased resistance, productivity, hardi-

ness, and feed efficiency
o Better yields of meat, eggs, and milk
o Improved animal health and diagnostic
methods

* Environment
o "Friendly" bioherbicides and bioinsecti-
cides
o Conservation of soil, water, and energy
o Bioprocessing for forestry products
o Better natural waste management
o More efficient processing

* Society
o Increased food security for growing
populations

Controversies

* Safety
o Potential human health impact: aller-
gens, transfer of antibiotic resistance
markers, unknown effects. Potential environmental impact: unintended transfer
of transgenes through cross-pollination,
unknown effects on other organisms (e.g.,
soil microbes), and loss of flora and fauna
biodiversity.

* Access and Intellectual Property
o Domination of world food production
by a few companies
o Increasing dependence on Industrial-
ized nations by developing countries

o Biopiracy—foreign exploitation of natural resources

* Ethics
o Violation of the intrinsic values of natural organisms
o Tampering with nature by mixing genes
among species
o Objections to consuming animal genes
in plants and vice versa
o Stress for animal

* Labeling
o Not mandatory in some countries (e.g.,
United States)
o Mixing GM crops with non-GM confounds labeling attempts

* Society
o New advances may be skewed to inter-
ests of rich countries

The term does not cover organisms whose genetic makeup
has been altered by conventional cross breeding or by "muta-
genesis" breeding, as these methods predate the discovery of
the recombinant DNA techniques. Technically speaking such
techniques are, by definition, genetic modification, though this
cross breeding is designated by lower case "g" and "m" not the
upper case GM of the recombinant DNA.
www.ornl.gov/sci/techresources/Human_Genome/home.sht-
ml

Grass Finished Animals, Grass-Fed or Pasture-Raised Cattle—Since 2000, several thousand ranchers and farmers across the United States and Canada have stopped sending their animals to the feedlots. Instead, they are keeping the animals home on the range and feeding them food that is as close as possible to their native diets. They do not implant the animals with hormones or feed them growth-promoting additives. (They are wormed and treated with conventional veterinary practices if there is a problem.) Animals grow at their normal pace. Animals raised on pasture live low-stress lives. As a result of their nutrition and lack of stress, they are healthy. When you choose products from pastured animals, you are eating food that nature intended. You are also supporting independent farmers, protecting small farms and rural communities, safeguarding the environment, promoting animal welfare, and eating food that is nutritious, wholesome, and delicious. For grass-fed beef, acorn fed pork contact <magruderranch@pacific.net> www.eatwild.com.

HEPA—An acronym for "high efficiency particulate air" filter, this type of air filter theoretically removes at least 99.97% of dust, pollen, mold, bacteria and any airborne particles with a size of 0.3 micrometers, at 85 liters per minute. The HEPA filter was designed in the 1940's and was used in the Manhatten Project to prevent the spread of airborne radioactive contaminants. It is a misconception that HEPA filters act like a sieve. HEPA filters work by:

1. interception, particles adhere to a fiber in the filter,
2. impaction, particles "run into" the filter or
3. diffusion, a behavior similar to Brownian motion. (The physical phenomenon where minute particles, immersed in a fluid or floating on its surface, move about randomly.)

www.aic.stanford.edu/health/hepa.html

Hormone Replacement Therapy (HRT) is a system of medical treatment for perimenopausal and postmenopausal women, based on the assumption that it may prevent discomfort and health problems caused by diminished circulating estrogen hormones. The treatment involves a series of drugs designed to artificially boost hormone levels. The main types of hormones involved are estrogens, progesterone or progestins, and sometimes testosterone.

HRT is available in various forms. It generally provides low dosages of one or more estrogens, and often also provides either progesterone or a chemical analogue, called a progestin. Testosterone may also be included. In women who have had a hysterectomy, an estrogen compound is usually given without any progesterone, a therapy referred to as unopposed estrogen therapy. HRT may be administered by patches, tablets, creams, gels or, more rarely, by injection. Dosage is often varied cyclically, with estrogens taken daily and progesterone or progestins taken for about two weeks every month or two; a method called sequentially combined HRT or scHRT. An alternate method, a constant dosage with both types of hormones taken daily, is called continuous combined HRT or ccHRT. It is a recent innovation. Sometimes an androgen, generally testosterone, is added to help reduce osteoporosis and to treat reduced energy and sexual desire (libido) after menopause. According to one friend who was taking ccHRT, "I became a 'She Bear'. I feel sorry for my husband. My intense libido surprised both of us!"

HRT is seen as either a short-term relief (often one or two years, usually less than five) from menopausal symptoms (hot flashes, irregular menstruation, fat redistribution etc.) or as a longer term treatment to reduce the risk of osteopenia leading to osteoporosis. Younger women with premature ovarian failure or surgical menopause may use hormone replacement therapy

for many years, until the age that natural menopause would be expected to occur.
www.nim.nih.gov/medlineplus

Kaya, Kayakalpa—Sanskrit, the term *Kaya* means "body" and *Kalpa* means "immortal". Kaya and Kayakalpa Yoga are ancient techniques of the Siddhas (saints) of South India for the enhancement of life energy. The Science of Kayakalpa delineates the manner in which the human body can be immortalized.

Restructuring the body in a natural way, Kaya and Kayakalpa help cure and prevent diseases. It relieves the practitioner of many of the troubles of aging. Kaya and Kayakalpa have a three fold objective:

1. Maintaining youthfulness and physical health,
2. Resisting and slowing down the aging process,
3. Postponing death until one reaches spiritual perfection.

Kaya and Kayakalpa give significant physical, mental as well as spiritual benefit by intensifying our life-force. Significant results have been observed in various types of chronic diseases and in overall improvement of general health. Kaya and Kayakalpa help cure and prevent diseases as well as relieve the practitioner of many of the troubles of aging. Specific actions include the stimulation of the brain cells to their highest functional levels, increase of memory power and cognitive ability, development of the immune system, reduction of the effect of hereditary diseases, reduction of the intensity of chronic diseases like hemorroids, diabetes, asthma and skin diseases, strengthening of the uterus and often, reduction of menstrual problems. Kaya and Kayakalpa are thought to bring about proper arrangement of polarity of body cells.

Labia—Labium (singular) a Latin term meaning "Lip". Labium and its derivatives (including labia, labial, labrum) are used to describe any lip-like structure. In the English language, labium often specifically refers to parts of the vulva.

Ligamentum Flavum—(singular: ligamenta flava) The *ligamenta flava* connect the laminæ of adjacent vertebræ, from top of the spine to bottom, from the axis to the first segment of the sacrum.

In the cervical region, the ligaments are thin, but broad and long; they are thicker in the thoracic region, and thickest in the lumbar region. As the ligamentum flavum descend and thicken, the range of motion decreases.

Their marked elasticity serves to preserve the upright posture, and to assist the vertebral column in resuming an upright position after flexion.

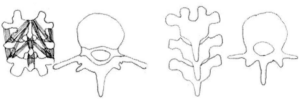

Lympathic System—The lymphatic system is a complex network of lymphoid organs, lymph nodes, lymph ducts, and lymph vessels that produce and transport lymph fluid from tissues to the circulatory system. The lymphatic system is a major component of the immune system.

The lymphatic system has three interrelated functions:

1. removal of excess fluids from body tissues,
2. absorption of fatty acids and subsequent transport of

chyle, a milky fluid formed in the small intestine during digestion of fats, to the circulatory system and

3. production of immune cells (i.e. lymphocytes and monocytes, and antibody-producing cells called plasma cells).

Lymph originates as blood plasma that leaks from the capillaries of the circulatory system, becoming interstitial fluid, filling the space between individual cells of tissue. Plasma is forced out of the capillaries by oncotic pressure gradients. As it mixes with the interstitial fluid, the volume of fluid slowly accumulates. Most of the fluid is returned to the capillaries by hydrostatic pressure gradients. The proportion of interstitial fluid returned to the circulatory system by osmosis is about 90% of the former plasma, with about 10% accumulating as overfill. The excess interstitial fluid is collected by the lymphatic system by diffusion into lymph capillaries, and is processed by lymph nodes prior to being returned to the circulatory system. Once within the lymphatic system the fluid is called lymph, and has almost the same composition as the original interstitial fluid.
www.wikipedia.org

Lymphedema—(American English), or "lymphatic obstruction", is a condition of localized fluid retention caused by a compromised vessels or nodes in the lymphatic system. The interstitial fluid of the body usually builds up in an arm or a leg. Lymphedema has been barely recognized as being a serious health problem; however, this is slowly changing due to education and awareness. The danger with lymphedema comes from the constant risk of developing an uncontrolled infection in the affected limb. Still, physicians and medical staff who practice in fields where this disease is uncommon may fail to correctly diagnose the condition due to the apparent lack of information regarding this disease.
www.stanfordhospital.com

Melatonin—a hormone found in all living creatures from algae to humans, at levels that vary in a diurnal cycle. In higher animals melatonin is produced by pinealocytes in the pineal gland (located in the brain) and also by the retina and GI tract. It is naturally synthesized from the amino acid tryptophan. (Remember the turkey dinner at Thanksgiving? And the napping? Tryptophan.)

Many biological effects of melatonin are produced through activation of melatonin receptors, others are due to its role as a pervasive and powerful antioxidant with a particular role in the protection of nuclear and mitochondrial DNA. Melatonin is also synthesized by various plants, such as rice, and ingested melatonin has been shown to be capable of reaching and binding to melatonin binding sites in the brains of mammals.

Production of melatonin by the pineal gland is under the influence of the suprachiasmatic nucleus of the hypothalamus (SCN) which receives information from the retina about the daily pattern of light and darkness. This signal forms part of the system that regulates the circadian cycle, but it is the SCN that controls the daily cycle in most components of the paracrine and endocrine systems rather than the melatonin signal (as was once postulated). Melatonin produced in the pineal gland acts as an endocrine hormone since it is released into the blood, whereas melatonin produced by the retina and the gastrointestinal (GI) tract acts as a paracrine hormone.
www.umm.edu/altmed/consSupplements/Melatonincs.html

When using a supplement, The Academy of Family Physicians recommends using synthetic melatonin because natural melatonin is made from the pineal gland of animals which could be contaminated with a virus.

Author's note: When taking a melatonin supplement for air travel or other circadian rhythm disruption, the smallest possible dose, (quartered) and for the shortest amount of time, seems to be most powerful. Melatonin supplements are often coated with an impermeable skin. Also, when purchasing supplements over the internet, Canadian products are required to maintain a higher standard of purity and rigorous testing than in the US. www.famliydoctor.org

Naturopathic Medicine—also known as naturopathy, is a school of medical philosophy and practice that seeks to improve health and treat disease by assisting the body's innate capacity to recover from illness and injury. Naturopathic practice include manual therapy, hydrotherapy, herbalism, acupuncture, counseling, environmental medicine, aromatherapy, nutrition, homeopathy and cell salts. Practitioners tend to emphasise a holistic approach to patient care. Naturopathy has its origins in the United States, but is today practiced in many countries around the world in one form or another, where it is subject to different standards of regulation and levels of acceptance.

Naturopathic Practitioner treat acute conditions such as headaches, sore throats, colds and flu, intestinal upsets, ear infections, contact dermatitis, urinary tract infections and sprains and strains. They treat for chronic illnesses such as migraine, autoimmune disease, cardiovascular disease, arthritis, cancer and musculoskeletal pain. They also treat mental and emotional problems such as stress, depression, anxiety and anger. They treat pregnancy and childbirth with extensive additional training. Licensed physicians from accredited schools are trained to use diagnostic tests such as imaging and blood tests before deciding upon the course of treatment. Naturopathic Practitioners employ prescription medications and minor surgery when necessary and often refer out to other medical practitioners. www.alternativemedicinechannel.com/naturopathic

Neti Pot—also *Jala neti* is an ancient Indian yoga technique, meaning literally "water cleansing", where the practitioner rinses out the nasal cavity with warm water (usually salted) using a neti pot. The technique is recognized by science under the term nasal irrigation.

Jala neti, though relatively unknown to western culture, is a common practice in parts of India and other areas in South East Asia, performed as routinely as using a toothbrush. It is performed daily usually the first thing in the morning with other cleansing practices. Sometimes it is done more often such as at the end of the day if you work or live in a dusty or polluted environment.

Osteopathic Medicine—formerly known as osteopathy, is "a complete system of medical care with a philosophy that combines the needs of the patient with current practice of medicine, surgery and obstetrics. The emphasis is on the interrelationship between structure and function. There is an abiding appreciation of the ability of the body to heal itself."

Doctors of Osteopathic Medicine, or DOs, apply the philosophy of treating the whole person (a holistic approach) to the prevention, diagnosis and treatment of illness, disease and injury using conventional medical practice such as drugs and surgery, along with manual therapy (Osteopathic Manipulative Medicine or OMM).

As with Doctors of Medicine (MDs), DOs educated in the United States are fully licensed physicians and surgeons who practice the full scope of medicine. Most DOs graduating outside the US are not medically trained practitioners. Currently, there are 24 accredited DO-granting osteopathic medical schools and 125 accredited MD-granting schools in the US.

MD and DO-granting US medical schools have similar curricula. Generally, the first two years are classroom-based, with certain programs providing patient contact, while third and fourth years consist of rotations through the different major specialties of medicine. Upon graduation, MD and DO physicians pursue residency training programs. Depending on state licensing laws, osteopathic physicians may be required to complete a one year rotating internship. Osteopathic physicians have the opportunity to pursue allopathic (MD) residency programs; however, the converse is not allowed. Within the US, osteopathic physicians practice in all medical specialties including, but not limited to, internal medicine, dermatology, surgery, radiology, etc. There is no distinction in pay between allopathic (MD) and osteopathic (DO) physicians, but physician salaries differ noticeably among the various medical specialties.

Osteopaths educated in countries outside of the US do not follow the same curriculum as US trained DO's. Their scope of practice is limited mainly to musculoskeletal conditions and treatment of some other conditions using OMM and various alternative medicine methods, not unlike chiropractors in the US.
www.wisegeek.com

Ovary—plural ovaries, are part of the vertebrate female reproductive system. A normal female will have two ovaries, each performing two major functions: producing eggs, or exocrine function and secreting hormones, or endocrine function. Ovaries in females are homologous to testes in males. The term gonads refers to the ovaries in females and testes in males. Most birds have only one functioning ovary; snakes have two, one in front of the other.

Oxytocin—Greek: "quick birth", is a mammalian hormone

that also acts as a neurotransmitter in the brain. In women, it is released mainly after distention of the cervix and vagina during labor, and after stimulation of the nipples, facilitating birth and breast-feeding, respectively. Oxytocin is released during orgasm in both sexes. In the brain, oxytocin is involved in social recognition and bonding, and might be involved in the formation of trust between people. Touch appears to produce small amounts of oxytocin.

Pericardium—a double-layered fluid-filled sac that contains the heart and attaches to the roots of the great vessels. The layers to this triple sac are the fibrous pericardium, the serous pericardium and the epicardium, considered a part of the heart wall.

The fibrous pericardium is the most superficial layer or outer layer. It is a dense connective tissue, protecting the heart, anchoring it to the surrounding walls and preventing it from overfilling with blood. It is continuous with the outer adventitial layer of the neighboring great blood vessels.

The serous pericardium is deep to the fibrous pericardium. It contains two layers, both of which function in lubricating the heart to prevent friction from occurring during heart activity. The layer next to the fibrous pericardium is the parietal layer. The layer next to the heart is the visceral layer.

Pilates Method—also called Pilates, is a physical fitness system that was developed in the early 20th century by Joseph Pilates.

Return to Life through Contrology and *Your Health: A Corrective System of Exercising That Revolutionizes the Entire Field of Physical Education* are two books he wrote about the system.

Pilates called his method *Contrology*, which refers to the way the method encourages the use of the mind to control the muscles. It is an exercise program that focuses on the core postural muscles that help keep the body balanced and are essential to providing support for the spine. In particular, Pilates exercises teach awareness of breath and alignment of the spine, and strengthen the deep torso muscles, which are important to help alleviate and prevent back pain.

Instead of performing many repetitions of each exercise, Pilates preferred fewer, more precise movements, requiring control and form. He designed more than 500 specific exercises. The most frequent form, called "matwork," involves a series of calisthenic motions performed without weight or apparatus on a padded mat. He, like the other practitioners you have been introduced to, believed that mental health and physical health were essential to one another. Pilates created what is claimed to be a method of total body conditioning emphasizing proper alignment, centering, concentration, control, precision, breathing, and flowing movement (The Pilates Principles) that results in increased flexibility, strength, body awareness, energy, and improved mental concentration.
www.pilatesmethodalliance.org

Precautionary Principal—states that if an action or policy might cause severe or irreversible harm to the public, in the absence of a scientific consensus that harm would not ensue, the burden of proof falls on those who would advocate taking the action.

The Precautionary Principle is most often applied in the context of the impact of human development or new technology on the environment and human health, as both involve complex systems where the consequences of actions may be unpredictable, even disastrous. Precautionary Principal is also applied to remediation of already existing industrial sites scheduled for conversion to malls and residential housing units.

The concept includes risk prevention, cost effectiveness, and ethical responsibilities towards maintaining the integrity of natural systems. The Precautionary Principal recognizes the fallibility of human understanding as a scientific certainty. It can also be interpreted as the transfer of more generally applied precaution in daily life (e.g. buying insurance, using seat belts or consulting experts before decisions) to larger political arenas.

As community members, we recognize that a stringent interpretation of the precautionary principle is advisable: proponents of a potentially harmful technology must show that the new technology is harmless before the new technology is used. www.globalcommunity.org

Proprioception— "the process by which the body can vary muscle contraction in immediate response to incoming information regarding external forces," by utilizing stretch receptors in the muscles to track joint positions in the body.

Proprioception and kinesthesia–the sensation of joint motion and acceleration–are sensory feedback mechanisms for motor control and posture. These mechanisms, with the vestibular system, the fluid network within the inner ear which keeps the body oriented and balanced, are unconsciously utilized by the brain to provide a constant influx of sensory information. The brain then sends immediate and unconscious adjustments to muscles and joints in order to achieve movement and balance.

Proprioceptors in the muscles monitor length, tension, pressure, and noxious stimuli. The muscle spindles, the most complex and studied of the proprioceptors, inform other neurons of the length of the muscle and the velocity of the stretch. The density of muscle spindles within a muscle increases in muscles involved in fine movements.

The brain requires information from many spindles in order to register changes in angle and position of the muscle and joints. There are also more spindles found in the arms and legs, in muscles that must maintain posture against gravity.

Another proprioceptor, the golgi tendon organ, is found where tendons meet muscles. They send information about the tension occurring in specific parts of the muscle. There are also proprioceptors sending information to the nervous system from joints and ligaments. Depending on the intensity of information, location in the body, and which proprioceptors are sending information, the brain will unconsciously or consciously process the information. In a healthy body, all input coming into the nervous system is processed.
-Thank you to Shannon Lee.
serendip.brynmawr.edu/bb/neuro/neuro02/web2/slee.html

Reflexology—a complementary therapy commonly called foot massage. Eunice Ingham developed Reflexology in the 1930s, based on earlier theory by Dr. William Fitzgerald known as "Zone Therapy". In 1913, Dr. Fitzgerald noted that specific parts of the body could have an anesthetic effect on another area. Developing this theory, he divided the body into ten equal vertical zones, ending in the fingers and toes. He concluded that pressure on one part of the zone could affect everything else within that zone.
www.reflexology.org

Rolfing, Ida Rolf, PhD, Structural Integration—The process known as *Rolfing* was developed in the early to mid

1950's by Ida Pauline Rolf (1896–1979). Rolf obtained her PhD in biochemistry in 1922.

Rolf claimed to have developed a method of organizing the human structure in relationship with gravity, which she originally called *Structural Integration of the Human Body.* Early consumers of Structural Integration coined the word *Rolfing* from the surname of Ida Rolf. Since the early 1970s, Rolfing has been a service mark of the Rolf Institute of Structural Integration, the school founded by Rolf.

According to Rolf, bound up fascia (or 'connective tissue') often restricts opposing muscles from functioning independently from each other, much as when water, having crystallized, forms the hard, unyielding ice. Her practice aimed to separate the bound-up fascia by deeply separating the fibers manually so as to loosen them up to allow effective movement patterns. Rolf states that an adequate knowledge of living human anatomy and hands-on training are required in order to safely negotiate the appropriate manipulations and depths necessary to free up this bound-up fascia. Advocates claim that after Rolfing, clients stand up straighter and gain in height, and bodily asymmetries of the soft tissue tend to disappear. Rolf's followers have produced photographic evidence of Rolfing's claimed effectiveness.

Rolfers prescribe a certain number of sequenced sessions to gradually "unlock" the whole body, often beginning with the muscles that regulate and facilitate breathing. Some people find the experience of Rolfing painful. Like surgery during the Civil War was quite crude by today's standards–though it saved lives, Rolfing has continued to evolve over the decades into a practice far more gentle than it was in its early origins.
www.rolf.org

Rosen Method Bodywork, Marion Rosen, PT. "This work is about transformation from the person we think we are to the person we really are."–Marion Rosen.

Rosen Method bodywork developed out of Marion Rosen's 50 years experience as a physical therapist and health educator.

In the 1930s, Marion studied breath and relaxation in Munich, Germany, with Lucy Heyer, who had been trained by Elsa Gindler, a renowned innovator of body therapies. Licensed in physical therapy, both in Stockholm and at the Mayo Clinic, Marion developed the Rosen Method over the course of many years in private practice in Oakland and Berkeley, Ca.

Rosen Method is distinguished by its gentle, direct touch. Using hands that listen rather than manipulate, the practitioner focuses on chronic muscle tension. As relaxation occurs and the breath deepens, unconscious feelings, attitudes, and memories may emerge.

The Rosen practitioner are trained to notice subtle changes in muscle tension and shifts in the breath. S/he recognizes these as indications that the client is relaxing and becoming more aware of his/her body and internal experience. The practitioner responds with touch and words which allow the client to begin to recognize what has been held down by unconscious muscle tension.

As this process unfolds, habitual tension and old patterns may be released, freeing the client to experience more aliveness, new choices in life, and a greater sense of well-being.

Thank you to Valerie Luotto, Karen Vinding and Marion Rosen.

www.rosenmethod.org

Sanskrit—a classical language of India, a liturgical language of Hinduism, Buddhism and Jainism. Sanskrit is one of 22 official languages of India.

It has a position in the cultures of South and Southeast Asia similar to that of Latin and Greek in Europe. Sanskrit is a central part of Hindu tradition and Philosophy. It appears in pre-Classical form as Vedic Sanskrit (appearing in the Vedas) with the language of the Rigveda being the oldest and most archaic stage preserved. This fact and comparative studies in historical linguistics show that it is from one of the earliest attested members of the Indo-European language family and descends from the same.

Today, Sanskrit is used as a ceremonial language in Hindu religious rituals in the forms of hymns and mantras. The corpus of Sanskrit literature encompasses a rich tradition of poetry and literature, as well as scientific, technical, philosophical and religious texts.

Sir William Jones, speaking to the Asiatic Society in Calcutta, February 2, 1786 said: *The Sanskrit language, whatever its antiquity, is of a wonderful structure; more perfect than the Greek, more copious than the Latin, and more exquisitely refined than either, yet bearing to both of them a stronger affinity, both in the roots of verbs and in the forms of grammar, than could possibly have been produced by accident; so strong, indeed, that no philosopher could examine them all three, without believing them to have sprung from some common source, which, perhaps, no longer exists.* www.omniglot.com

Savasana or Shavasana—"Corpse Posture", is a yoga asana (posture) used to conclude a yoga session. It is a mix of relaxing postures designed to rejuvenate one's body, mind and spirit.

While shavasana is a good way to reduce stress and tension, it is not recommended for meditation as it has a tendency to induce sleepiness. If afflicted by drowsiness or restlessness of the mind while performing shavasana, increase the rate and depth of breathing.

Sensory Motor Amnesia—a condition in which the sensory-motor neurons of the voluntary cortex have lost some portion of their ability to control all or some of the muscles of the body. Thomas Hanna estimated that perhaps as many as fifty percent of the cases of chronic pain suffered by human beings are caused by sensory-motor amnesia (SMA).

Sensory motor amnesia occurs as a functional deficit whereby the ability to contract a muscle group has been surrendered to sub-cortical reflexes. These reflexes will chronically contract muscles at a programmed rate. The voluntary cortex is powerless to relax these muscles below that programmed rate. It has lost and forgotten the ability to do so.

Muscles held chronically in partial contraction will predictably become sore or painful; become weak with constant exertion; cause clumsiness because of their inability to coordinate synergetically with overall bodily movements; cause a constant energy drain of the body; and create postural distortions and poor weight distribution that will cause secondary pain typically mistaken for arthritis, bursitis, herniated discs, and so on.

These symptoms of SMA are commonly misdiagnosed by traditional health care practitioners, for they attempt to treat them by intervening mechanically or chemically in the local musculoskeletal areas affected. Such local intervention has no lasting effect upon the symptoms, inasmuch as it treats a functional problem of the brain as if it were a structural problem of the peripheral body. The result is chronic pathology that cannot be successfully treated by traditional health care. The condition seems medically incurable, leaving no option but the use of analgesic drugs that only mask the symptoms.

The condition of SMA, so little understood and affecting such a large portion of the population, can be remedied by only one means: a reeducation of the voluntary sensory-motor cortex. The cortex must be reminded sensorially of what it has forgotten so that, once again, it has full motor control of the muscular areas affected. When it does so, the symptoms mentioned above disappear, and the chronic, medically incurable situation is alleviated.

SMA can only be overcome by education, not by treatment. An internal process must occur whereby new sensory information is introduced into the sensory-motor feedback loop, allowing the motor neurons of the voluntary cortex once again to control the musculature fully and to achieve voluntary relaxation.
www.somatics.com/hannart.htm

Siddha Vaidya—meaning "subatomic medicine" is possibly the oldest health and longevity system providing time-honored remedies for prevention of illness of the body.   Siddha Vaidya defines health as a complete presence of physical, mental, emotional, spiritual and social balance.

Siddha Vaidya recognizes eight branches of medicine, the same branches recognized by western medicine except geriatrics, the medicine for the aged. Instead rejuvenation and regenerative therapy is named as a branch of medicine. The aim of this therapy is to maintain the youth of the individual along with long life. This is attainable through detoxification of the body and rejuvenation treatments which activate the innate ability of the body to rebuild and renew itself. www.indianmedicine.nic.in/html/siddha/siddha.htm

Sodium Lauryl Sulfate—Sodium dodecyl sulfate (SDS or NaDS) (C12H25NaO4S), also known as sodium lauryl sulfate (SLS), is an ionic surfactant that is used in household products such as toothpastes, shampoos, shaving foams and bubble baths for its thickening effect and its ability to create a lather.

It appears that there are two quite differing views on the safety of using and exposing the body to constant low levels of toxic chemicals such as Sodium Lauryl Sulphate (SLS). Some people are affected by SLS and its derivatives more than others. It is suspected that SLS is linked to a number of skin issues such as dermatitis. When combined with certain chemicals, SLS may become a carcinogen. SLS is commonly used in research laboratories as the standard skin irritant with which other substances are compared. There are over 150 different names by which SLS and its derivatives are known. Although SLES is slightly less irritating than SLS, the liver is unable to metabolize SLES. Low cost is the prime reason SLS is used in many soaps, shampoos, washing powders, toothpastes and other bathroom products. SLS is known to cause aphthous ulcers, commonly referred to as "canker sores".

Soft Tissue—In medicine, the term *soft tissue* refers to tissues that connect, support, or surround other structures and organs of the body. Soft tissue includes muscles, tendons, fibrous tissues, fat, blood vessels, nerves, and synovial tissues. Often soft tissue injuries are some of the most chronically painful and difficult to treat because it is very difficult to see what is going on under the skin with the soft connective tissues, fascia, joints, muscles and tendons.

Musculoskeletal specialists and neuromuscular physiologists and neurologists specialize in treating injuries and ailments in the soft tissue areas of the body. These specialized clinicians often develop innovative ways to manipulate the soft tissue to speed natural healing and relieve the mysterious pain that often accompanies soft tissue injuries. This area of expertise has become know as *Soft Tissue Therapy* and is rapidly expanding as the technology continues to improve the ability of these specialists to identify problem-areas more quickly.

Somatics—Somatic disciplines are often referred to as body-work, body therapies, hands-on work, body-mind integration, body-mind disciplines, movement therapy, somatic therapy, movement awareness or movement education or somatic education. Somatic disciplines involving movement as a fundamental part of the learning process are part of the field of somatic movement education and therapy.

   • case histories illustrate "the myth of aging" and the concept of "sensory-motor amnesia";

   • the theory and research underpinning sensory-motor amnesia based on studies from the fields of cognitive-behavioral psychology, kinesthesiology, and medical science;

   • somatic exercises facilitate the re-integration of sensory-motor awareness and reverse chronic pain and rigidity due to sensory-motor amnesia.
www.somatics.org

Synesthesia—(also spelled *synæsthesia* or *synaesthesia*, plural *synesthesiae*) — from the Greek *syn*, meaning union and *aesthesis*, meaning sensation — is a neurological condition in which two or more bodily senses are coupled. In a form of synesthesia known as *grapheme alpha color synesthesia*, letters or numbers may be perceived as inherently colored, while in a form of synesthesia called *ordinal linguistic personification*, numbers, days of the week and months of the year evoke personalities which are consistently evoked over considerable time intervals.

While cross-sensory metaphors are sometimes described as *synesthetic*, true neurological synesthesia is involuntary and occurs in slightly more than four percent of the population. It runs strongly in families, possibly inherited as an X-linked dominant trait.

Many people with synesthesia use their experiences to aid in their creative process, and many non-synesthetes have attempted to create works of art that may capture what it is like to experience synesthesia. Psychologists and neuroscientists study synesthesia not only for its inherent interest, but also for the insights it may give into cognitive and perceptual processes that occur in everyone, synesthete and non-synesthete alike. www.medterms.com

Unani Medicine—Arabic for *Ionian*, means "Greek." It is a formal medicine that has been practiced for 6,000 years. Also known as *hikmat*, Unani Tibb Medicine was developed by the Greek physician Hippocrates (40 – 370 B.C.) from the medicine and traditions of the ancient Egypt and Mesopotamia. When the Mongols invaded Persia and Central Asia, many scholars and physicians of Unani fled to India.

Unani Tibb is practiced today among Muslims of Xinjiang, China. It is part of Uighur medicine in India, Pakistan, Bangladesh and Sri Lanka. Unani Tibb is rooted in the understanding that spiritual peace is essential for good health.

Hikmat defines the body in terms of the four humors or akhlaat: air, earth, fire and water emanate from the liver which then forms a subtle network around the body. Similar to Siddha Vaidya, Ayurveda and the Chinese traditions, foods and herbs are also classified according to the humors. The four humors correspond to four bodily fluids: blood, phlegm, black bile and yellow bile.

A typical diagnosis of a patient would take the balance of these humors into consideration. For example, over-stimulation of wet-hot elements effects nervous biochemical interactions within the body including glandular ramifications within the blood. A wet-cold over-stimulation also effects nervous biochemical interactions but with ramifications for the relationship between the muscular biochemical exchanges and the bloodstream such as diarrhea and diabetes. Excess black bile in the blood leads to heart palpitations and constipation while excess yellow bile leads to general weakness.

Hikmat/Unani further defines the state of the body into three different stages: health, disease and neutral. Neutral in the physical body means the state between health and disease when symptoms have not yet manifested. Disease occurs when the functions associated with the vital, natural, and psychic forces of the body are obstructed or unbalanced due to deviations. Hikmat/Unani also divides the body into seven natural and fundamental components defined as: a) arkan – elements b) mizaj – temperament, c) a'da – organs, d) ruh – vital forces, e) quwaat – energy and f) af'al – action. Any loss or change in any one of these components is considered a major factor in disease or death.

Hikmat/Unani also considers the external environment and its effect on the body. The theory divides these influences into five categories. It is believed that each of these five categories must be fulfilled adequately for a person to be able to maintain a proper balance in the four humors and proper state of balance. The external environment and daily lifestyles influences considered as major factors in the ability to sustain and maintain good health are:

1) The air of one's environment
2) food and drink
3) movement and rest
4) sleep and wakefulness and
5) emotions.

Hikmat/Unani states that these factors should be balanced in quality, quantity and sequence in order to sustain good health and a natural life based in faith.

As Rasulullah informed us "Allah has sent down both the disease and the cure and He has appointed a cure for every

disease, so treat yourselves medically, but use nothing unlawful"
(Sunan abu Dawud, 28:3865).

Beyond diagnosis and categorization skills, hikmat contributed
many other clinical skills to the field of medicine. Practices
evolved to include brain surgery, laparotomy and plastic surgery. Thus, hikmat became divided into branches of medicine
that covered internal medicine, surgery, gynecology, obstetrics,
pediatrics, toxicology, psychiatry, rejuvenation therapy, sexol-
ogy, diet therapy and hydrotherapy.
  Hikmat sees illness as an opportunity to serve, clean, puri-
fy and balance the physical, emotional, mental and spiritual
planes. Towards this goal, hikmat therapies are natural. Unani
Tibb therapies include appropriate fresh food in order to correct the imbalances, herbal medicines, minerals, the promotion
of codes of conduct conducive to positive health, and appropriate rest as prevention and cure. Unani Tibb also emphasizes
compounds that belong to the human body and the avoidance
of allergy-producing foods.

  Healers who are educated in the hikmat method of healing
are also given unique instructions to follow with their clients
and in their clinics. These unique requirements stem from the
Islamic faith.
  www.islamonline.net

Upledger, John D. DO, OMM—originated CranioSacral
Therapy after conducting scientific studies at Michigan State
University from 1975 to 1983 where he served as a clinical
research and Professor of Biomechanics. CST is a gentle hands-
on treatment which evaluates and enhances the craniosacral
system. A touch of no greater than 5 grams, the weight of a
nickel, releases restriction found in the membranes and cere-
brospinal fluid surrounding and protecting the brain and spinal

cord. Successful treatment associated with pain and dysfunction include migraine headaches, chronic neck, back pain, and shoulder pain, Temporomandibular Joint Syndrome (TMJ) and shoulder pain.
www.upledgerclinic.com

Vagina—The vagina, (from Latin, literally "sheath" or "scabbard") is the tubular tract leading from the uterus to the exterior of the body in female placental mammals and marsupials. In common speech, the term "vagina" is often used inaccurately to refer to the vulva or female genitals generally; strictly speaking, the vagina is a specific internal structure and the vulva is the exterior genitalia only.

Valgus—in orthopedics, a valgus deformity is a term for the outward angulation of the distal segment of a bone or joint. The opposite of valgus is called varus.

Varus—in orthopedics, a varus deformity is a term for the inward angulation of the distal segment of a bone or joint. The opposite of varus is called valgus.

For example, in a varus deformity of the knee, the distal part of the leg below the knee is deviated inward, resulting in a bow-legged appearance. Conversely, a valgus deformity at the knee results in a knock-kneed appearance, with the distal part of the leg deviated outward.
"varus = inward" and "valgus = outer" and always refers to the direction that the distal part of the joint points.

Vipassana—(Pali) or vipasyana (Sanskrit) means to see things as they really are, insight. It is one of India's most ancient techniques of meditation. The technique involves quiet sitting while observing respiration. It was rediscovered by Gotama Buddha more than 2500 years ago and was taught by him as a universal remedy for universal ills, i.e., an Art Of Living.

This nonsectarian technique aims for the total eradication of mental impurities and the resulting highest happiness of full liberation. Healing, not merely the curing of diseases, but the essential healing of human suffering, is its purpose.

Vipassana is a way of self-transformation through self-observation. It focuses on the deep interconnection between mind and body, which can be experienced directly by disciplined attention to the physical sensations that form the life of the body, and that continuously interconnect and condition the life of the mind. It is this observation-based, self-exploratory journey to the common root of mind and body that dissolves mental impurity, resulting in a balanced mind full of love and compassion.

The scientific laws that operate one's thoughts, feelings, judgments and sensations become clear. Through direct experience, the nature of how one grows or regresses, how one produces suffering or frees oneself from suffering is understood. Life becomes characterized by increased awareness, non-delusion, self-control and peace.
www.dharma.org

Virabhadrasana—Sanskrit for Warrior Pose. Named for a fierce warrior, an incarnation of Shiva, both Warrior I and II strengthens legs, opens hips and chest and stretches arms and legs. Virabhadrasana develop concentration and stillness, responsible attributes for real warriors. Use these poses or asanas, to stay in present time. Balance on both feet, lifting off the pelvic frame, keeping the tail relaxed and the head floating on the axis and atlas of the spine, shoulders lowered and relaxed.

Healing Actions for Big Body Matters

www.catwinternational.org

The Coalition Against Trafficking in Women is a feminist human rights nongovernmental organization that works internationally to promote a world in which women's rights are human rights, where prostitution and sex trafficking do not exist; where women are free and equal in dignity and rights; where no woman is sexually exploited; that recognizes and values the great genius of women in the development of civilization and cultures; where women have sexual integrity and autonomy.

www.heifer.org

Heifer International transforms entire communities by gifts of animals and training in sustainable farming techniques.

www.grameen-info.org

Grameen Bank (GB) has reversed conventional banking practice by removing the need for collateral and created a banking system based on mutual trust, accountability, participation and creativity. GB provides credit to the poorest of the poor in rural Bangladesh, without any collateral. At GB, credit is a cost effective weapon to fight poverty and it serves as a catalyst in the over all development of socio-economic conditions of the poor who have been kept outside the banking orbit on the ground that they are poor and hence not bankable. Professor Muhammad Yunus, the founder of "Grameen Bank" and its Managing Director, reasoned that if financial resources can be made available to the poor people on terms and conditions that are appropriate and reasonable, "these millions of small people with their millions of small pursuits can add up to create the biggest development wonder."

www.globalexchange.org

Global Exchange is a membership-based international human rights organization dedicated to promoting social, economic and environmental justice around the world.

www.newdimensions.org

New Dimensions produces broadcast dialogues and other quality programs that explore creative solutions to urgent challenges facing humankind.

www.pesticides.org

The Northwest Coalition for Alternatives to Pesticides protects the health of people and the environment by advancing alternatives to pesticides.

Author's note: cancer in children is increasing while adult cancer is decreasing. There appears to a direct correlation between the increase of childhood cancer and exposure to toxins with pesticide being a major source of these cancer causing toxins.

www.pnhp.org

Physicians for a National Health Program

The US spends far more on health care per person than any other nation. Yet we have lower life expectancy than most other rich countries. Every other advanced country provides all its citizens with health insurance; only in America is a large fraction of the population uninsured or under insured. Educate yourself. We need to have this conversation and we need to have it now.

www.sierraforestlegacy.org

Sierra Forest Legacy protects and restores the ancient forests, wildlands, wildlife, and watersheds of the Sierra Nevada through scientific and legal advocacy, public education and outreach, and grassroots forest protection efforts.

Index

Notes

Darca Lee Nicholson lives in Northern California where she has a private practice in integral health care. She teaches yoga at Mendocino College and Yoga Mendocino. She regularly visits Ft. Worth, Texas, Philadelphia, Pennsylvania and Trivandrumn, Kerala, South India, where she teaches and continues to study and learn.

www.darcaleenicholson.com

Peaceful Touch, The Power of Touch

The power of touch is miraculous in its simplicity. It is a necessary gift of nature, without which a human being cannot thrive. Peaceful Touch programs integrate healthy touch into children's activities, from games and story-telling to reading, math, and science. In Sweden, where more than 300,000 children practice Peaceful Touch on a regular basis, both teachers and parents report lower levels of anxiety and aggression, and improved group functioning.
Fundamentals

The Peaceful Touch program is based on three fundamentals:

* * That touch is necessary for human growth and development*
* * That the calming hormone, oxytocin, is activated through touch*
* * That a permission process supports healthy touch and helps establish good boundaries*

Working together like the three legs of a stool, these fundamental concepts support the integrity of the Peaceful Touch program.

www.peacefultouch.net